RONALD REAGAN
OUR 40TH PRESIDENT

RONALD REAGAN
OUR 40TH PRESIDENT
★ ★ ★ ★
WINSTON GROOM
BESTSELLING AUTHOR OF *FORREST GUMP*

Regnery
1947 | **75**YEARS | 2022
WASHINGTON, D.C.

Copyright © 2012 by Winston Groom

All rights reserved. No part of this publication may be reproduced or transmitted in any form or by any means electronic or mechanical, including photocopy, recording, or any information storage and retrieval system now known or to be invented, without permission in writing from the publisher, except by a reviewer who wishes to quote brief passages in connection with a review written for inclusion in a magazine, newspaper, website, or broadcast.

Regnery® is a registered trademark and its colophon is a trademark of Salem Communications Holding Corporation

Library of Congress Cataloging-in-Publication Data

Groom, Winston, 1944-
  Ronald Reagan : our fortieth president / by Winston Groom.
    p. cm.
  Includes bibliographical references and index.
  ISBN 978-1-59698-795-1 (alk. paper)
  1. Reagan, Ronald. 2. Presidents--United States--Biography. 3. United States--Politics and government--1981-1989. I. Title.
  E877.G76 2012
  973.927092--dc23
  [B]
                    2012000175

Published in the United States by
Regnery Publishing
A Division of Salem Media Group
Washington, D.C.
www.Regnery.com

Manufactured in the United States of America

2022 printing

Contains material reprinted with the permission of Simon & Schuster, Inc. from AN AMERICAN LIFE by Ronald Reagan. Copyright © 1990 Ronald W. Reagan. Reprinted by permission of Nancy Reagan.

Every good faith effort has been made in this work to credit sources and comply with the fairness doctrine on quotation and use of research material. If any copyrighted material has been inadvertently used in this work without proper credit being given in one manner or another, please notify the publisher in writing so that future printings of this work may be corrected accordingly.

Books are available in quantity for promotional or premium use. For information on discounts and terms, please visit our website: www.Regnery.com.

To Theron Raines, my literary agent, who originated this book, and shepherded it all the way through.

CONTENTS

CHAPTER ONE
Welcome to the White House, Mr. President 1

CHAPTER TWO
The Boy from Tampico 9

CHAPTER THREE
Joe College 17

CHAPTER FOUR
On the Air 27

CHAPTER FIVE
There's No Business like Show Business 37

CHAPTER SIX
Lieutenant Reagan, U.S. Army 47

CHAPTER SEVEN
The Political Conversion of Ronald Reagan 57

CHAPTER EIGHT
A Reversal of Fortunes 67

CHAPTER NINE
The New Sun 75

CHAPTER TEN
Mister President..87

CHAPTER ELEVEN
A Blink between Life and Death...97

CHAPTER TWELVE
Star Wars and the Evil Empire...107

CHAPTER THIRTEEN
Changing the Rules of the Game...119

CHAPTER FOURTEEN
"Then I Was Gone"..129

CHAPTER FIFTEEN
The Last Stand on Earth...141

READER'S GUIDE..149

BIBLIOGRAPHY..153

INDEX...155

CHAPTER ONE

WELCOME TO THE WHITE HOUSE, MR. PRESIDENT

When Ronald Reagan first walked into the Oval Office after being elected president, there was already a daily agenda sitting on his desk.

It was not always this way.

The first day Abraham Lincoln entered the White House in 1861, as the nation teetered on the brink of civil war, he was greeted with these unsettling words from outgoing President James Buchanan: "If you are as happy entering this house as I am leaving it, then you must be the happiest man in the country."

Seventy-two years later, when Franklin D. Roosevelt first arrived at the White House in the midst of the Great Depression that was threatening to ruin the country, he rolled his wheelchair around from room to room shouting, "Where *is* everybody!" And in fact nobody was there.

Twelve years later, Vice President Harry S. Truman, who was suddenly pitchforked into the Oval Office by Roosevelt's death while World War II was still raging, declared, "If you've ever been hit by a load of hay, then you know just how I feel!"

Ronald W. Reagan's first day was nothing like those others. Gone were the days when a president could walk in and have some time to get accustomed to how things worked, to how his days might go. There were already meetings and briefings scheduled by the staff, which Reagan noted in his famous diary in an almost cursory fashion.

But the issues Reagan faced on that first day, and in the days to follow, were in many ways far more dangerous and critical to America than any of the matters dealt with by previous U.S. presidents. What was at stake was not only the fate of the United States, but possibly the fate of the world—in other words, its destruction by atomic weapons. It took a man of stern moral character to meet those challenges and, luckily, Ronald Reagan was such a man.

★ ★ ★

When we speak of character, we mean those moral and ethical qualities that define one's personality. Traits such as honesty, integrity, determination, courage, graciousness, leadership, humor, reliability, and intelligence, or some combination of these, define an outstanding individual. Likewise, character may show itself in the *absence* of certain undesirable features, such as dishonesty, cowardice, pettiness, sloth, rudeness, or cruelty. And especially in their presidents, the American people have come to believe that character counts.

Since 1789, when George Washington was elected the first president of the United States, forty-four men have served in the office. Most of them were of high moral character. Some were not. Some were effective *despite* certain character flaws, such as meanness, untruthfulness, jealousy, sourness, indecision, shortsightedness, drunkenness, and stupidity. Others were not.

Unlike many countries, America puts a high price on character as a precondition for our elected officials—above all, for the office of president. In fact, Americans demand it. In the past, the voters have made a few mistakes in their choice of leaders, and lived to regret them. But when in 1980 they elected Ronald Wilson Reagan the fortieth president, whether one agreed with his politics or not, it was impossible for any serious person to question his character.

Reagan was a charismatic personality who soon acquired the nickname "The Great Communicator" for his ability to relate to the American people in speeches and interviews. The fact that he had once been a Hollywood movie star did not hurt him in this, but what most people immediately saw in Ronald Reagan was a no-nonsense guy who had bootstrapped himself up from poverty to the highest office in the land with a sense of humor, intelligence, and toughness.

To history's profit, Reagan was one of the rare presidents to keep a daily diary while in office. (The last one to do so had been President Rutherford B. Hayes, 1877–1881.) This record allows us to see history in the making, the way Reagan himself saw it, one day at a time. The entries disclose a man of candor, wit, and even shrewdness when it came to difficult situations, confirming there is no artifice between the public Ronald Reagan people saw on television and the man himself, as revealed in his own words.

★ ★ ★

One might best describe Reagan as a "skeptical optimist"; he would have made a formidable poker player if he'd been so inclined. He was never a "hands-on" president who fiddled with every detail, and certainly no "workaholic." On Inauguration Day he was asleep in his bedroom when an aide knocked on the door at 9:00 a.m. to remind him the ceremony was in two hours.

"Does that mean I have to get up now?" Reagan replied innocently. He'd meant it as a joke, but when the press got hold of it they played the story as though he'd been serious and made fun of him. Once, when a reporter questioned the brevity of his office hours, Reagan replied,

"Well, I know they say hard work never killed anybody—but why take the chance?" The media made fun of him for that, too.

Today we often hear Reagan described as "beloved," but in fact during his presidency he was frequently the target of the same snide, mean-spirited, often uninformed attacks as the rest of the modern presidents—or for that matter, practically all presidents since George Washington. Outwardly he shrugged this off, and while it would probably gratify some to hear that inwardly it pained him greatly, the fact was that it didn't. His diaries and his conversations recounted by those who knew him indicate that at worst, while he might have become annoyed by his antagonists, he seemed to have such a steady and sunny disposition that he would simply write off nasty criticism as bad form or wrong-headedness—a fact that further infuriated his enemies, since they always hoped to "get his goat" and were angry and felt cheated.

Reagan's major achievement of course—and this nation and the world should remain eternally grateful for it—was that he, personally, was more responsible than anyone else for bringing down the Iron Curtain and causing the collapse of Soviet Communism and the threat it posed, including the distinct possibility of world destruction. Many of his critics have belittled his role in this, but the record is clear.

★ ★ ★

From the moment he reached the White House, Reagan faced formidable challenges left to him by previous administrations. Monetary inflation was running at the ghastly rate of 12 percent a year. In a nutshell, what that meant was that in another eight years the value of a dollar earned and saved in or before 1981, the year he was inaugurated, would be worth exactly zero. The prices on almost everything had skyrocketed, and people weren't earning enough to keep up. If inflation couldn't be curtailed, the country faced the possibility of another Great

Depression, in which countless millions would be left jobless, homeless, and destitute.

At the same time, interest rates—the amount of money charged by banks to borrow money—had spiraled out of control to a shocking 18 to 20 percent of the borrowed amount per year. This meant that ordinary people could no longer afford to take out loans for their houses or automobiles, and the same held true for businesses, which depended on borrowing money to finance their purchases.

The price of gasoline was $1.35 a gallon—which would be about $3.40 a gallon today, when adjusted for inflation—because of a dramatic increase in the price of oil by a monopoly of mostly Islamic countries in the Middle East, Africa, and Asia. People were feeling the strain in everything from car travel to airfares to the price of home heating oil.

In short, the U.S. economy when Ronald Reagan took over was in shambles.

★ ★ ★

Worse, America's role as a world power had become dangerously eroded.

When the U.S. emerged from World War II, it was the strongest military force on earth, thanks to the atomic bomb. Unfortunately, the great Communist cabal of the Soviet Union—headquartered in Russia—soon began to challenge us for world domination. They stole the secrets of the bomb, aided by Soviet spies in England and among our own citizens.

Determined to spread Communism throughout the world, the Soviets and their ally, Communist China, having already taken most of Eastern Europe and much of the Far East, began meddling in South and Central America and the Caribbean, where Cuba had been turned into a Soviet satellite state. If the Soviets could get a firm hold in South

America, it would become a dangerous step in their plan to strangle the world's great democracies.

Ever since the end of World War II, the United States and its allies Great Britain and the nations of Western Europe had been engaged in what was called the "Cold War" against the Communist powers. Sometimes it turned into "hot" war, as in Korea and Vietnam, when the U.S. and other democratic countries sent troops to fight against a Communist takeover.

But the most serious danger lay in the Soviet buildup of nuclear missiles, aimed at the United States and the other democracies. If a nuclear war had somehow started, it would have been the end of life on earth as we know it. Ironically, the world was kept at nuclear peace simply by adhering to a chilling doctrine known as Mutually Assured Destruction (MAD), which held that if atomic war broke out, there could be no winners, because the exchange of missiles would destroy both sides.

MAD, however, only worked so long as the United States—by far the most powerful nation among the western democracies—was able to keep enough nuclear missiles pointed at Russia to deter the Communists from starting a war with any hope of winning it. And that is where the trouble was, when Reagan took office.

From the mid-1960s to the early 1970s, the United States had fought a costly, controversial, and losing struggle to keep the Communists from taking over the nation of South Vietnam and the rest of Southeast Asia. Nearly 60,000 American servicemen had been killed in seven years of fighting, and in the end the U.S. and its allies pulled out, paving the way for the Communists in North Vietnam to absorb their southern neighbor.

The war left a bitter taste in everyone's mouth. The Republican administration of President Gerald Ford had presided at last over the Vietnam defeat, and the Washington politicians were in no mood to vote large sums of money for military spending. Soon the U.S. armed forces began to deteriorate.

The situation grew dramatically worse under President Ford's successor, Jimmy Carter, a Democrat who had graduated from the U.S. Naval Academy. During Carter's single term in office, he neglected the military to the extent that American warships often could not sail, and warplanes could not fly, due to lack of spare parts and trained technicians. The defense budget had been so slashed that there was often insufficient fuel and ammunition for training purposes. Morale in the military plummeted. It was even reported that some military families were on food stamps.

At the same time, while the United States had apparently forsaken its armed forces, the Soviet Communists had undergone a spectacular military buildup, and now exceeded the U.S. with more than twice as many warplanes, five times as many tanks and armored vehicles, and fourteen times as many artillery pieces.

Scariest of all was the missile gap. On the day Ronald Reagan took office, the Soviets had enough atomic missiles aimed at cities across the United States not only to destroy half the U.S. population, but also, in Reagan's own words, "to destroy virtually all of our own missiles on the ground." Thus the doctrine of MAD—Mutually Assured Destruction—had become merely a good idea that was no longer a reality.

Few at the time (including the Communists) realized the danger America was in, and Reagan certainly did not publicize it; instead he began immediately and desperately to do something about it.

★ ★ ★

This, then, was the perilous strategic situation that Ronald Reagan faced when he was sworn into office at the U.S. Capitol on a cold January day in 1981.

There was, however, a bit of good news.

International terrorism had not quite yet reared its ugly head the way we know it now, but was only in its formative stages. One of those stages, however, had arrived more than a year earlier in the shape of a mass kidnapping of fifty-four American diplomats in the U.S. embassy in Iran by several hundred Islamic fanatics. This was totally in violation of international law and diplomatic practice. However, the kidnappers held the Americans hostage to protest what they said were American misdeeds against Iran, which had recently fallen under the strict Islamic control of the Ayatollah Khomeini, who denounced the United States as the "Great Satan."

The hostage-taking was embarrassing, making the U.S. appear powerless to protect its own people. In some corners of the world America was held up as a "pitiful, helpless giant," especially after the Carter administration bungled an attempt to land a military force in the Iranian desert to rescue the hostages. Negotiations—involving embargoes, threats, concessions, and ransom—seemed to go nowhere until, on the day Carter left office and Reagan was sworn in as president, the hostages finally were set free. The reasons will probably never be entirely understood.

The hostage release was one of the few pieces of good news to come Reagan's way as he began to absorb the enormity of the challenges and dangers he would have to deal with. A man of lesser character might simply have pulled down the shades and gone back to bed, but Reagan did no such thing. He was sixty-nine years old, and no spring chicken, but he set to work to rectify the dismal problems that stared him in the face. He made mistakes during his eight years in office, some of them serious, but no one can say that he didn't give it all he had. That was his character.

CHAPTER TWO

THE BOY FROM TAMPICO

American presidents have been born in log cabins, mansions, hospitals, and various places in between, but Ronald Reagan seems to be the only president who was born above a saloon. This event occurred in Tampico, Illinois, on a cold February day in 1911, and when he came into the world his father took one look at him and said, "He looks just like a fat little Dutchman." The image stuck; for the rest of his life Reagan's close friends called him "Dutch."

Tampico is a small farming town way out in the prairies west of Chicago, where the land is as flat as a table and tornados roar through so often they call it "tornado alley." Even the local newspaper is called *The Tornado*. In the Spanish language, Tampico means "place of the otters"; the town apparently got its name because before farmers began digging drainage ditches in the 1850s, much of the land was flooded and it was said that many otters lived there.

Reagan grew up poor, but didn't really know it. Sometimes when times were hard, he and his brother, Neil (who was two years older and nicknamed "Moon"), ate what their mother called "oatmeal meat," which she would fix by mixing a pot of oatmeal with some hamburger and gravy. Reagan thought it was a perfectly good, normal meal until he got older and found out otherwise.

His father, Jack, was a shoe salesman whose grandfather had come to America during the terrible Irish Potato Famine in the 1840s. Jack kept the Irishness and "the gift of blarney" of his forebears. "No one I ever met could tell a story better than he could," Reagan said of his father. On the other hand, Jack was somewhat cynical by nature, and defensive about being Irish… and poor Irish at that.

Those were the days when hotels often posted signs saying, "No Theatricals [actors] or Irish," and this led Jack to a stern commitment against prejudice of any sort. Once, on a shoe-selling trip, he arrived at a hotel where the desk clerk told him Jews were not permitted as guests. Jack picked up his suitcase and left, telling the clerk, "I'm a Catholic. If it's come to the point where you won't take Jews, then some day you won't take *me* either." Unfortunately, it was the town's only hotel, and Jack spent the night in his car during a roaring blizzard.

But because of incidents like that, the Reagan household was free of bigotry, and the Reagan boys were encouraged to make friends with all people and treat them as equals. It was made clear to them from the time they were small that blacks, Jews, or anyone else were welcome in their home, and racial slurs or intolerance of any kind were strictly forbidden. It was an instructive lesson Reagan carried with him to the end of his days.

There was, however, a dark side to Reagan's father. He was a drunkard. He wasn't habitually drunk, but sporadically went on binges, during which he could be difficult for his family and others. Sometimes there would be loud arguments, and slamming of doors, or his father would disappear for days at a time. His mother always told the boys that their father had an "illness" and shouldn't be blamed for it. But it remained an embarrassment. Sometimes Dutch and Moon were bundled up without explanation and hustled off to spend a few days with an aunt or uncle. It was only much later that they understood why.

One snowy evening when Dutch was about ten, he came home from the YMCA and was stunned to find his father flat on his back, passed out drunk in the snow. Despite his chagrin and subsequent anger, he somehow managed to haul his father into the house and get him to bed. Furthermore, he never said anything about it to his mother, but the incident left an indelible impression.

Oddly enough, Jack's drinking sprees did not occur on those frequent occasions when things were going badly, as when his shoe store business fell through, or when he lost his job on Christmas Eve. Instead, he seemed to take to the bottle when things were going well, almost as if he did not want to succeed. Jack Reagan lived in a world of broken dreams, and his personality was self-defeating, as though something inside told him he would never rise above his class—he was just poor Irish, the way his ancestors had been for many generations.

So, as if he was trying to make this prophecy self-fulfilling, whenever things began looking up, he grabbed a bottle to bring them down. Some good did come of this, though: like so many children who find traits they dislike in their parents, throughout his life Ronald Reagan seldom drank alcoholic beverages.

In contrast to her husband, Reagan's mother, Nelle, was a saint. She was a deeply religious woman, always busy as a bee, and of course started Dutch and Moon in Sunday school and church at an early age.

Even though they were poor, and she often had to take in sewing or even other peoples' washing to make ends meet, Nelle was constantly looking to help people even poorer than she was, down to and including prisoners in the county jail. By all accounts she was bright and cheerful, and she impressed that outlook on her two sons. This goes far in explaining Dutch's temperament as he grew into adulthood. Unlike his father, who tended to be cynical and usually thought the worst of people, Dutch developed a trusting, easy-going, good-natured personality, and was unfazed by criticism or slights. He did not let himself become discouraged by defeats, and was always ready to take advantage of a good opportunity—attributes that served him well when he entered politics.

Nelle Reagan was also a dedicated reader and dramatic performer, though she'd never finished grade school. In those days most people didn't even have radios, and at night she would read to the Reagan boys. On other occasions, as a star member of the town's dramatic group, she would perform "readings" from famous poems, books, speeches, or plays, and that was where young Ronald first got his flair for acting and the theater.

When he was nine or ten, his mother persuaded him to memorize a short speech and deliver it to the dramatic club, which he did, despite his shyness and not a little stage fright. "I don't remember what I said," he recalled much later, "but I'll never forget the response: *People laughed and applauded.*" He was hooked.

Because of his father's occupation (as well as his drinking), the family moved a lot. They never owned a home, but always rented—sometimes a house, but usually an apartment. Just about the time Dutch began making friends in one town, it would come time to move; probably because of this, Dutch became pretty independent, which is another way of saying he was a bit of a loner.

With the exception of a short stay in Chicago, the places where Jack Reagan moved his family were more or less like Tampico: small, rural Midwestern farming towns where conservative Christian values were stressed. Dutch came to love sports, but he wasn't very good at them. When he'd try to catch an easy fly in baseball, invariably it would go over his head, or fall in front of him, or he'd drop it. And at bat—forget it. He was game enough, but when it came to choosing teams, Dutch Reagan was usually picked last.

One day, when he had just entered his teens, they discovered the reason. Jack Reagan had taken the family on a Sunday drive. In those days, it was a common practice after church and "Sunday dinner" to just pile the family into the car and ride around looking at things. When you passed someone else, you always waved. Dutch and Moon were in the back seat when Dutch found his mother's eyeglasses and decided to try them on. Then he "let out a yelp." A whole new world had opened up. Suddenly he could see the leaves on trees, the pictures on billboards, and what a moment before had been merely an undefined mass of black and white turned out to be a herd of dairy cattle.

The glasses they got him fitted with were big, thick, and ugly. Dutch described them as "monstrosities." But he wore them anyway; he had no choice, and he accepted it. Later, after he became a football star in high school and college, he would tell people, "I couldn't play baseball because I couldn't see good enough. That's why I turned to football. The ball was bigger, and so were the fellows."*

When Dutch turned thirteen he entered Dixon High School in Dixon, Illinois. It was 1924, and America was more or less prospering. Even Jack Reagan had found good work in a shoe store and was able to move the family into a nice rented house "on the right side of the tracks." The world, also, was more or less at peace, following the end of the Great War, as World War I was known then, which had drenched the earth with blood from 1914 to 1918.

Ever since he could remember, Dutch Reagan had felt a passion for playing football. Even though he was short and scrawny, he joined the sandlot games with the other kids. But now as the leaves began to turn and the nights grew chilly in the long, golden Midwestern autumn, he dreamed of playing on a real team, with real uniforms, before a real

---

* James C. Humes, *The Wit and Wisdom of Ronald Reagan* (Washington, D.C.: Regnery Publishing, Inc., 2007).

crowd that packed the stands on Friday nights or Saturday afternoons in small towns like Dixon and Tampico to cheer their teams along.

The coach sized him up. Dutch was 5'3" and weighed 108 pounds, hardly big enough to play tiny mite football, but he was given a practice uniform anyway (they had to find a special pair of pants small enough to fit him), and he took his place on the scrimmage field among the other boys, most of whom outweighed him by at least fifty pounds. When the time came to post the game roster, Dutch's name wasn't on it. A lesser boy might have given up and joined the band, or become a cheerleader or a team manager, but it wasn't in the nature of Ronald W. Reagan to quit that easily. He immediately "determined to make the team during my sophomore year." Which he did.

This was before the days of weight rooms and exercise machines to build muscles, so Dutch got a job the next summer on a construction gang. It not only helped his physique, but it allowed him to put some money in the bank, a practice that followed him all through high school and college. He understood early on, and cheerfully so, that if he was going to make anything of himself in life, he would have to earn it.

That year he made the junior varsity and was elected captain of the team, playing tackle and guard—what today are described uncharitably in the coaching business as "non-skill" positions. But Dutch loved the physical contact of the line, the blocking and tackling, and next year, when he had shot up to nearly six feet and weighed 160 pounds, he made the varsity.

Still, during the first several games he sat on the bench, until one day the coach became "unhappy" with the first string guard and put Dutch in the game. And he stayed on first string in every game for the rest of the season and next season too, his senior year. Once he got put in, Reagan remembered long afterward, he was determined to "never let the other guy [get] his position back."

Beginning with his discouraging freshman year, Dutch had turned disappointment into triumph by the time he graduated. What it taught him was that it took hard work, perseverance, and a belief that if you tried, had faith in yourself, and kept at it, good things would result. It was another of life's stern but hopeful lessons, learned young, and it was ingrained in the character of Ronald Reagan for the rest of his life—especially, when he would need it most, as president of the United States.

CHAPTER THREE

JOE COLLEGE

Football was only one of Reagan's passions during his high school years. In fact, one wonders where he found the time for his many interests and activities. For one thing, he was a dedicated reader, his favorites including *The Rover Boys*, the Tarzan books by Edgar Rice Burroughs, Jack London's *The Call of the Wild*, and later *Frank Merriwell at Yale* and *Brown of Harvard*. It is interesting, even touching, that he found these last two stories so appealing, given that in his present situation he had about as much chance of going to Yale or Harvard as he did of becoming president of the United States. But unlike so much of today's fiction, the books Reagan read featured genuine heroes who performed deeds that were noble and exciting, and a boy could dream, couldn't he?

Jack Reagan had always told his sons that if they wanted to go to college they had best start saving their money, because he didn't believe he could ever afford to pay for it himself, and such things as student loans didn't exist back then. Thus in 1926, when Reagan was fifteen, he found "one of the best jobs I ever had." It was as a summer lifeguard on Dixon's sparkling clear Rock River that ran through the Lowell wildlife sanctuary, the most popular swimming place in town. Because he was a standout swimmer and had taken a course in lifesaving at the YMCA, the city paid him $15 a week for ten- to twelve-hour days, and he managed to save most of it for college. He kept that job every summer until he was twenty-two years old, and the only thing that made him prouder than putting on the sleeveless singlet that had "lifeguard" stenciled on it, was the fact that during those years he saved the lives of seventy-seven people.

While he definitely had no ear for music, Reagan nonetheless joined the town boys' band as a drum major. He enjoyed telling the story about the time they were performing in a nearby town on Decoration Day (honoring the soldiers of the First World War, now known as Memorial Day). Reagan was doing some fancy high-stepping out in front of the band, pumping his baton, dressed in his "white ducks, bright tunic and high, beaked hat," when he suddenly realized he didn't hear band music anymore. He looked back to find he was completely alone. The band had vanished.

Apparently the parade marshal had turned his horse around and led the band down a side street, which was the planned parade route. Reagan dashed through backyards, alleys, and cross streets until he finally found the parade again and fell into step in front of his band. Later in life he used the incident to illustrate why some people claimed that he often "marched to the beat of a different drummer."

Even if he wasn't musical, Reagan was decidedly artistic in other ways. For one thing, he discovered he was good at drawing, beginning as a doodler, and going on to cartoons. In fact he thought at one point he might be able to make a career as a cartoonist.

More significantly Reagan began, on his own, in the evenings or other private times, to write short stories. Like many of the books he read, his plots frequently centered on football, or the recently ended war, and the settings were often Ivy League schools such as Yale and Harvard that had captured his imagination from his reading. His stories are compact and well-crafted, and many of his passages demonstrate a talent usually found only in accomplished writers—the ability to convincingly put *himself* into the different characters he was imagining, so that it appeared he was actually *living out* the various roles. He didn't share the stories with others much though, but apparently wrote them privately for himself. It was many years later that they were discovered, and are now part of the collection at the Reagan Library.

Most important, by his senior year Reagan was heavily involved in the two activities that would wind up shaping his entire adult life. First, he was elected student body president, and second, he joined the drama club and developed a passion for acting.

A great deal of his fascination with acting had to do with a new English teacher at Dixon High, whom Dutch credited with showing him things about acting "that stayed with me for the rest of my life." The teacher, B. J. Frazer, was young, short, and, according to Reagan, wore eyeglasses "almost as thick as mine." His way of teaching was completely different from Reagan's previous teachers. Where in the past student essays had been graded only on the basis of grammar and spelling, Frazer announced that he also was going to grade essays on their "originality." Reagan took this new challenge to heart, and before long Frazer had him reading his essays aloud to the class. This, in turn, invoked appreciation and laughter from his fellow students, which prompted Reagan to try out for a school play.

It happened that Mr. Frazer was also the drama coach and stage director. He had abandoned the customary practice of having the student actors merely get up and read essays or perform individual scenes from old, stale plays. Instead he acquired scripts from the latest Broadway shows and had his students act them out from beginning to end, with the whole school (and parents, too) for an audience.

As with the essay writing, Frazer's approach to stage directing was radically different from the previous teacher's. Instead of telling the students to say a line in a particular way, he would prompt them to ask themselves what a particular character *meant* when he said a certain line—what that character was *thinking*. Reagan immediately saw the reasoning behind this method, which was to get the actors *inside* the minds of the characters they were playing, and it came naturally to him, because he'd already done it in his short story writing.

In the end, Reagan said he became "so addicted to student theatrical productions that you couldn't keep me out of them."

And to make the picture complete, by now he had fallen in love.

She was named Margaret Cleaver and was, by Reagan's description, "short, pretty, auburn-haired and intelligent." She was also the daughter of the new minister at Reagan's church, which was soon to cause trouble from a quarter he had not anticipated.

Nelle Reagan had raised her sons in Christ Church, a fundamentalist Protestant offshoot, and not long after Reagan and Margaret began dating, Margaret came to him in distress. Jack Reagan, it seemed, had just gone on one of his drunken sprees, and word of it had gotten around town, including to the teetotaling Cleaver household who, along with most of the congregation, were religiously strict and considered drinking one of the greater sins. Margaret had somehow gotten a full account of Jack Reagan's disgraceful behavior, and it presented her with both an emotional and a religious conflict to be going out with the son of the town drunk.

Naturally, Reagan was mortified. He tried to explain it to Margaret the way his mother had explained it to him: that his father's problem was a "sickness" and should be forgiven, but according to Reagan, Margaret "didn't buy it."

It caused real heartbreak in the Reagan household. Reagan went to his mother, who counseled patience with his father, but Reagan was so much in love he was ready to disavow his father and not speak to him again, ever. These were tense moments that only a teenager can fully appreciate. Here Reagan was in love with a girl he believed he would some day marry, and his father's misbehavior was threatening to ruin the relationship. As good luck would have it, Margaret saved it herself after some soul searching of her own. She concluded that their romance was more important than Reagan's father's drinking.

Nevertheless, it must have weighed heavily on Reagan's mind. Here was someone he loved very much—his own father—whose selfishness (Jack Reagan apparently didn't buy the "sickness" line either) had nearly broken up his first love affair with a nice, beautiful girl. Likely, it left him feeling he was in a very lonely place, with nowhere to turn.

★ ★ ★

In those days, only a small percentage of the U.S. population actually graduated from high school, and of those who did, only 7 percent went on to college. Most dropped out along the way to work, usually at what were called "blue collar" jobs. Moon Reagan was one of these. He believed college was a waste of time, and took a job in a cement factory in Dixon.

But Ronald was different. He always seemed to be different. He wanted more, seemed to sense that *more* was his portion, that he was going places. Where, he didn't yet know, but he sure didn't intend to be a failed drunken shoe salesman like his father.

As it happened, Margaret Cleaver had chosen to enroll at Eureka College, a small liberal arts school about a hundred miles south of Dixon, and when Reagan drove her there in the autumn of 1928, he was "bowled over" by the charming Georgian-style campus, with ivy-covered buildings, verdant lawns, and tall, stately trees.

Reagan would also be the first to tell you that he wasn't thinking of getting a college education there, so much as he was thinking of Margaret's being there and something else that was almost as important: football.

Eureka (Greek for "I have found it!") had a respectable football team in those days, which, while it played mostly small schools, also had on its schedule such teams as Illinois State and Western Michigan. It had always been Reagan's dream to play college football, since he rued the final game of his high school season as the last one he would probably ever play.

Unfortunately, though he'd saved practically every dime he'd earned as a lifeguard, it still wasn't enough to get him through school, so while Margaret registered, Reagan went in unannounced to see the president of the school, and made the best case he knew to get a scholarship for football. He even threw in swimming on Eureka's swim team as an added attraction.

This approach worked, and between the small scholarship the college was able to offer, waiting tables at a fraternity house, and his savings from lifeguard days, Ronald Reagan became a freshman at Eureka College. It was heaven.

Waiting on the tables at the frat house wasn't exactly so bad, because with the help of the boyfriend of one of Margaret's sisters, Reagan actually received and accepted a bid to join Tau Kappa Alpha, or TKE, the largest college social fraternity in America. And it was customary for the pledges to wait on tables their freshman year, in exchange for free meals. It was notable that Reagan selected TKE—or rather that they selected him—because unlike many college Greek societies, TKE had been founded on the principle of equality among men, instead of selecting members on the basis of wealth and social status. This was true, too, of the college itself. Eureka had been established in 1857 by the leader of a wagon train of Disciples of Christ, abolitionists who had headed west from slaveholding Kentucky, looking for a better world.

Two events stood out in Reagan's first year in college. First, he sat on the bench during the entire football season, just as he had as a freshman in high school, fuming, because he thought the coach had it in for him. Second, he led a successful strike by the entire student body to force out a new president who was undermining Eureka's academic credibility in the name of financial austerity. The student strike and the resulting national publicity associated with it gave Reagan his first inklings of "activism," which was usually associated with labor organizations or left-wing causes. But the strike's success showed him the empowerment that the "little fellows"—people who are presumed to be under a higher authority—can achieve if they stand united.

Sitting on the bench during football games, however, just wouldn't do. Reagan brooded about it all during his summer life-guarding season at Rock River, and finally decided he wasn't going back to Eureka. But when Margaret's family drove her down to school for her sophomore year, Reagan decided to go along for the ride, if for nothing else than to say goodbye to his college friends.

He hadn't been on campus more than a few minutes when he realized what a mistake it would be to drop out. There was the smell of autumn in the air and the promise of football games on brisk Saturday afternoons, and the friendships he'd made, and then of course there was Margaret. He hadn't been there twenty minutes before he'd talked the school authorities into giving him a job "cleansing silver" (washing dishes) in the girl's dormitory, which was enough to cover his expenses. Dutch Reagan was back.

Had he not made that decision, there's no telling where Reagan's life would have taken him. It might have been to comfortable wealth and achievement in some field or other. Or it might have been to the assembly line at the Ford Motor Company's plant in Detroit. Who can say?

But he *did* make the decision, and wound up starting and starring in practically every football game for the next three years. He joined the college drama society and starred in that, too, providing him the working tools he'd need when he finally got to Hollywood.

Once, during an out-of-town football trip, the team had to put up in Reagan's hometown of Dixon. But when they got to the hotel there, the desk clerk told the coach, "I can take everybody but your two colored boys." The coach said they'd go to another hotel, but there wasn't one that would take in blacks. Dutch had a suggestion: "Why don't I take them to my home?"

The coach gave him "a funny look," and asked if he was "sure he wanted to do that?" Reagan said he was, and so he and the two black kids arrived at the Reagan household. Nelle answered the door, and Dutch told her there wasn't room at the hotel for the whole team, and so he'd brought these guys home to bunk with them.

"'Well come on in,' she said, her eyes brightening with a warmth felt by all three of us." They may have been poor, and Jack may have been the town drunk, but there was no hatred, no bias, and certainly no hint of racial discrimination in the Reagan family home.

In the meantime, the stock market crash of 1929 during Dutch's sophomore year precipitated the Great Depression, which was to last for more than a decade, and at its worst leave more than 25 percent of Americans unemployed. At times Reagan had to send what little college money he could spare to his mother to keep the family going, but somehow, like most Americans, they managed to muddle through.

During his Christmases home from college, his parents couldn't even afford a Christmas tree, but his mother would always decorate something—a cardboard box, a table—with colorful ribbons to give the place "a festive feeling." And Moon, Dutch, and their parents always managed to find enough change to buy little gifts for each other. It wasn't much, but Christmas was Christmas; you couldn't just ignore it, even if there was a Depression on.

Despite all of this, during Reagan's remaining years at Eureka, he managed to letter in football, track, and swimming, was an editor of the student yearbook, served two terms in the student senate, and his senior year he campaigned for and was elected president of the student body. He graduated with a "gentleman's C," majoring in economics, and set out following the summer of 1932, at the height of the Depression, to forge his own brave new world.

Meantime, he gave Margaret Cleaver an engagement ring.

CHAPTER FOUR

ON THE AIR

After receiving his degree from Eureka, Reagan returned to Dixon and his final stint as a summer lifeguard at the Rock River beach. Though he had majored in economics, his real aspiration was to become a movie star. But if he had said that to anybody in Illinois in 1932, during the worst of the Great Depression, he would have made himself look ridiculous.

What he *did* believe he could do, however, was something he considered the next best thing, which was to become a radio sports announcer. It made perfect sense; he lived and breathed sports, and had gained a real dramatic flair from all of his drama classes and acting in plays. So when the lifeguard season was over, Reagan hitchhiked the hundred-odd miles to Chicago, the Mecca for radio in the Midwest.

Radio in those days was almost as big as the movies. There were no televisions then, and radio was filled with programs that everyone listened to just as avidly as people now watch the daytime TV talk shows and soap operas and the nighttime newscasts, sitcoms, and dramatic series. Radio was wildly popular for live sporting events, especially football and baseball games. Sports announcers in particular had to have the gift of smoothly portraying in words a perfect picture of what was going on at every moment during a sportscast. It was crucial to be able to convey excitement, disappointment, elation, and any other mood, along with routine happenings on the field. Silence was not an option, even for time-outs, halftimes, inning changes, etc. Radio was what Reagan later called the "theater of the mind."

Chicago was home to affiliates of the two big radio networks, CBS and NBC, as well as the big power station WGN, and a host of smaller ones, and Reagan eagerly went to their stations seeking an audience. Soon, however, he began to realize a hard fact: nobody was interested in a recent college grad with no radio experience, who had played football and studied acting. His final interview confirmed this, when a woman with the NBC station heard him out and then told him, "You are going about this the wrong way. Go out in what we call the sticks. Try to get a job with one of the smaller stations. They're often willing to give a newcomer a chance. Then come back and see me after you have some experience."*

It was disheartening, the more so because Reagan didn't have much money and needed a job, any job, and soon. He thumbed back to Dixon in the rain, getting a number of rides, including one unsavory lift from a man who trapped skunks for a living, tasting the bitter gall of defeat.

When he got home, however, there was good news waiting: his father told him that Montgomery Ward, the huge Chicago department store and mail order house, was opening a store in Dixon and looking for someone to manage the sports department. Even better, they wanted the person they were looking for to have been prominent in local high school

---

* Ronald Reagan and Richard Gibson Hubler, *Where's the Rest of Me?* (New York: Duell, Sloan, and Pearce, 1965).

sports. It was good pay and steady work that promised promotions, and if anyone fit the bill, it was Reagan.

Or so he thought. Three days after he made his formal application they turned him down in favor of a former Dixon High basketball star. Meanwhile, Margaret Cleaver had managed to find a teaching job in a remote part of the state, and would soon be leaving town. Their engagement was now much less promising than it had once seemed. This was the low point in his life so far.

Reagan needed to find work in the worst possible way, and a few days later began a strange little odyssey that would carry him to Davenport, Iowa, and, though he could not know it at the time, eventually to Hollywood and movie star fame, the governorship of the largest state in the Union (by population), and finally to the presidency of the United States.

★ ★ ★

Reagan decided to follow the advice of the woman who'd talked with him at NBC in Chicago, and began visiting small radio stations "out in the sticks," to see if anyone would take him on. Davenport happened to be home to a small station called WOC, which stood for World of Chiropractic, because it was owned by a local chiropractor.

The program manager for WOC was a feisty Scotsman named Peter MacArthur, who had toured America in a vaudeville performing troupe until he became so crippled by arthritis that he sought out the Davenport chiropractor who owned the station. There wasn't much to be done about the arthritis, but because of his stage talent, the chiropractor offered MacArthur a job as an announcer, and later made him program director.

MacArthur was about to dismiss Reagan until he learned that his main interest was becoming a sports announcer, and that he had played football in high school and college. He asked Reagan if he thought he could go into the sound studio right then and broadcast a fictitious college football game, "and make me *see* it as if I was home listening on the radio?"

Reagan said he would give it a try. He closed the door, sat down at the mike, and began broadcasting what he recalled of the fourth quarter of the Eureka-Western State University game—which in fact he'd played in last season—a game Eureka had won in the final seconds. When he was finished, he had a job. It was only a temporary job, announcing Big Ten games on Saturday afternoons at $10 a pop ($150 today), but at least it was a start, and Reagan was determined to learn and improve and make a name for himself in the sportscasting business.

But when football season ended, so did his job. There was no regular opening yet at WOC.

Languishing in Dixon and waiting for something to turn up, Reagan confronted a situation that would leave a deep impression on him throughout his later political life. In fact, it might have been the earliest inkling of his eventual transformation from a political liberal to a conservative. He mentioned it in his autobiography, and it's probably worth repeating here.

Because of Jack Reagan, the family had always been staunch Democrats; Reagan once even speculated in jest that he had been confirmed at birth into the Democratic Party. He was a great admirer of Franklin D. Roosevelt, and remained one even after his own switch from liberal to conservative.

During the Depression, his father had managed to get a job running the local branch of Roosevelt's Works Progress Administration, which was a new agency set up to help find employment at government expense for the many men who were without jobs. His father found that the men, many of whom were his friends, were all eager to work whenever they were offered the opportunity. But this soon began to run afoul of programs administered by the welfare bureaucrats who had been sent out from Washington to give direct money handouts to the needy.

The problem was that whenever the welfare people found out Jack Reagan had secured a temporary job for somebody, they cut that person and his family off from welfare and made reapplying for it an almost impossible ordeal.

His father was furious and, in one of the few times that he went on a binge when things were going badly, took to the bottle for a few days before sobering up and going back to the office.

Reagan, however, saw his father's dilemma clearly, and it became the basis of his long-standing opposition to welfare handouts, or "relief" as it was known. He recalled that Roosevelt himself had declared: "To dole out relief...is to administer a narcotic, a subtle destroyer of the human spirit.... The Federal government must and shall quit this business of relief."

Then Reagan made an observation that became a mantra for his entire political career: "But it didn't work out that way.... Wheels were turning in Washington and government was busy at the job it does best—growing."

It was maddening for Reagan, watching the men coming to his father for work, and then slowly but surely as the welfare people took control, fewer and fewer of them came, until most stopped coming at all. His father, he said, never forgave the government for preventing men from making an honest dollar in favor of welfare handout money, but he also recalled that his father always blamed the local government people—never the Roosevelt administration or Congress, or the growing bureaucracy in Washington.

Reagan later recalled that Roosevelt had run on a platform of monetary responsibility and cutting out wasteful and useless programs. And he remained convinced that had it not been for pressing international problems, including World War II, Roosevelt would have resisted this great expansion of government that occurred during his long term in office. But Reagan also noted, "As smart as [Roosevelt] was, though, I suspect even FDR didn't realize that once you created a bureaucracy, it took on a life of its own. It was almost impossible to close down a bureaucracy once it had been created."

★ ★ ★

The call from Pete MacArthur finally came two months later, early in 1933; a regular announcer's job had opened up at WOC, and of course Reagan leapt at it. It did not last long, however, owing to Reagan's forgetting to give on-air credit to a Davenport funeral home for the playing of organ music they had sponsored. He was removed as a regular announcer and put back on temporary duty as a sports-only broadcaster.

But that did not last long either, because soon WOC was absorbed into the big fifty-kilowatt WHO radio station of Des Moines, Iowa, an NBC affiliate. Now Reagan was given opportunities to be heard all over the Midwest. He took full advantage of this, and during the next four years became one of the most popular sports commentators in Middle America, covering scores of important college football games, track meets, swimming events, and baseball.

His baseball coverage provides one of the best known and most delightful of the Reagan stories. In those days, many radio stations pulled off something of a scam on their listeners. When a game was played out of the listening area, a station would save paying sportscasters travel money by getting them to call the game anyway—but from their own studio—by using reports sent via open telegraph wire from a telegrapher at the game.

From WHO's studio in Des Moines, Reagan "covered" hundreds of Chicago Cubs and Chicago White Sox baseball games in this fashion—sitting in the control room across from a telegrapher named "Curley," who received play-by-play reports from the Western Union telegrapher who was actually *at* the game. Quickly deciphering each coded message, Curley would slip notes of the action to Reagan through a slot in a glass barricade.

But on one such occasion, Reagan found his imagination "taxed to the maximum," as he recalled it. The Chicago Cubs were playing the St. Louis Cardinals and the score in the ninth inning was still 0 to 0. Reagan was doing his act of pretending to be in the press box at Wrigley Field, when suddenly a note came under the glass that said: "*The wire's gone dead.*"

Stunned, Reagan shot a glance at Curley, who only shrugged with his palms up.

The wire had gone out right in the middle of a pitch thrown by the St. Louis great, Dizzy Dean, to the Cub's shortstop, Billy Jurges.

Reagan might have missed a beat, but only one. He immediately decided to carry on a charade until the wire was fixed and, in his own estimation, gave the greatest impromptu performance of his career.

Jurges, he told the listeners, had hit the ball foul. He then described boys in the stands fighting over the foul ball. Next he had Dizzy Dean refuse the catcher's signs over and over.

The wire remained dead.

Reagan began describing the weather, then the manager coming out to the mound to confer with Dean. He described another foul ball. He announced that there was another fight in the stands. He kept having Jurges hit foul balls for a full seven minutes—so many, that the incident was reported as a record to "Ripley's Believe It or Not."

When the wire finally came back on, the first note Curley slipped to Reagan was that Jurges had been put out on an easy pop-up fly from Dean's first pitch. Reagan then picked up where he had left off, and to his eternal pride, nobody was any the wiser.

★ ★ ★

It was during this time that Reagan's engagement to Margaret Cleaver fell through. They hadn't been able to see each other much, what with him in Iowa and her being in a remote part of Illinois. They wrote frequently of course, but two years after Reagan moved to

Des Moines, a letter came that included his engagement ring and fraternity pin.

Margaret, it seemed, had fallen in love with a Foreign Service officer while on a cruise to Europe with one of her sisters. Reagan was heartbroken for a while, but finally chalked it up this way: "Our lovely and wholesome relationship did not survive growing up." Later he concluded that what had saddened him most was "not so much... because she no longer loved me, but because I no longer had anyone to love."

As luck would have it, about this time something else came into Reagan's life that would offer him a lifetime of love and enjoyment, and that was horses.

Ever since he'd been a little boy, watching cowboy serials at the local movie matinees, he'd dreamed of riding horses. During his lifeguard days back in Dixon, he'd ridden a little bit on someone's borrowed horse, and sometimes he and friends would rent horses at a stable in Des Moines for Saturday morning rides. But a horse—especially a good horse—was a very expensive thing to keep.

Then one day he learned that the U.S. Army's 14th Cavalry Regiment, based outside Des Moines, was offering commissions to young college-educated men who would agree to go through a rigorous officers' training program.

Reagan was not seized by any deep patriotic compulsion to enter the Army. After all, the "War to End All Wars" had only ended fifteen years earlier. But the chance to become an Army officer with unlimited access to some of the best cavalry horses in the world was too good to turn down.

It took two years of study and field problems on weekends, but in 1937 he was finally commissioned a second lieutenant of cavalry in the U.S. Army. That same year Adolf Hitler allied with Italy's fascist dictator Benito Mussolini to form the Axis Powers, which would be joined by Japan, who had withdrawn from the League of Nations and begun attacking her neighbors in Asia.

The dark clouds of war may have been rising over Europe and the Orient, but for now Reagan was having the time of his life. In the Midwest at least, he was near the top of his profession, and had cemented his love of horseback riding into a lifelong passion. He was an excellent rider, too, thanks to his U.S. Cavalry training, and he was fond of the old saying, "There is nothing better for the inside of a man, than the outside of a horse."

CHAPTER FIVE

THERE'S NO BUSINESS LIKE SHOW BUSINESS

For two years, Reagan had been going out to California for the Chicago Cubs spring training on Catalina Island off the Los Angeles coast. Both the team and the island were owned by the Wrigley chewing gum family.

As the long, dreary Iowa winter dragged into February, Reagan again convinced the WHO management to send him to California, but this time he had an ulterior motive, and it had nothing to do with baseball or sports announcing.

A girl he knew who'd once been with WHO was now the lead singer of a big dance band, and a bit-part player in movies. Once in Hollywood, Reagan took her to dinner between shows and let it drop that he wanted to get into acting.

"I know an agent who will be honest with you," she told him. "If we're wrong, and you should forget the whole idea, he'll tell you." She added, "And before you see him, take off those glasses!" Reagan thought that last line was funny, because without his glasses, he said, "I couldn't see him at all."

But next morning Reagan was sitting across the desk from the talent agent Bill Meiklejohn, embellishing his acting credentials on the theory that "a little lying in a good cause wouldn't hurt." Finally Reagan asked Meiklejohn bluntly, "Should I go back to Des Moines and forget this, or what do I do?"

Meiklejohn calmly picked up the phone and called the casting office at the Warner Brothers studio.

"Max, I have another Robert Taylor sitting in my office," he informed Warner's famous casting director, Max Arnow, referring to one of the top movie stars of the day.

"God made only one Robert Taylor," was Arnow's indifferent reply.

Nevertheless, within the hour Reagan found himself in Meiklejohn's car on the way to Warner Brothers where, in his own words, he was welcomed "like a piece of prize beef": measured, poked at, photographed, sized up. A screen test was shot, with Reagan doing a scene from Philip Barry's play, *Holiday*. Next morning, he got on the train with the Chicago Cubs, and returned to Des Moines.

He'd hardly unpacked when a telegram came from Bill Meiklejohn:

WARNERS OFFERS CONTRACT SEVEN YEARS STOP ONE YEAR OPTION STARTING $200 A WEEK STOP WHAT SHALL I DO MEIKLEJOHN

"*Sign before they change their minds*," Reagan hastily replied.

Then he let out a yell. It was 1937. He was twenty-six years old and about to be in the movies. It was the chance of a lifetime—a dream come true.

★ ★ ★

Two hundred dollars a week was a lot of money, assuming he worked every week. It wasn't movie star rich, but it was certainly good money by any measure, especially at the height of the Depression. For the first few weeks, Reagan was dancing on air. Everybody he knew was glad for him, especially his parents and Moon, who were beside themselves. He took the time to break in a new announcer at WHO, then said his goodbyes.

One of the first things Reagan did was buy a car. All his life his family could only afford used cars, but now he picked out a brand new Hudson convertible. It wasn't as elegant or expensive as, say, a Packard or a Cord, but with white sidewalls and a V-8 engine, it was plenty spiffy. It was in this that he set out for California in the late spring of 1937, across the amber fields and purple plains, the mountain majesties and barren deserts, bound for Hollywood.

The morning after he arrived, he drove out to the Warner Brothers lot in Burbank, where he got his first taste of film-making. It wasn't what he expected. Suddenly nothing about him, it seemed, was satisfactory. They took him into makeup, where someone remarked that his hair looked like it had been cut by putting a bowl over his head. Then they decided his head itself was too small for his wide shoulders, and that his neck was too short. He would look funny on screen, was the consensus. They ordered narrow shoulder jackets for him and sent him to James Cagney's shirtmaker, who knew how to make special collars for men with short necks. They showed him how to make a big double-Windsor knot in his tie, which would give the appearance of shrinking the distance between his shoulders.

Then they led him over to publicity, which objected to his name. He was seated at a table with a number of Warner's press agents, who immediately began suggesting what his stage name should be. Somebody would make up a name, the others would shake their heads, then the process would be repeated, while Reagan sat there like a bump on a log, feeling silly.

Finally he made an observation of his own. "May I point out," he said, "that I have a lot of name recognition in a large part of the country, particularly in the Middle West, where I've been broadcasting sports. I think a lot of people would recognize my name on theater marquees." The others looked at each other, nodded, and so was born Ronald Reagan, movie actor.

His first movie, a few days later, was tailor-made, so to speak. It was called *Love Is on the Air*, and he played—what else—a radio announcer. After a day's rehearsal they began shooting. All morning he'd had the jitters, but as soon as the director said "action," he found himself completely lost in the scene. To his astonishment, the director said he was happy with the first take and moved on to the next shot. A few months later, *Love Is on the Air* was released, to relatively good reviews. By then Reagan had been cast in another picture (typecast again, in the role of a cavalryman), then another, and was comfortably ensconced as a "B-movie" player at Warner's.

In those days of the "studio system," everyone started out in B-movies. The B's were low-budget films that would get second-billing on a double-feature that always included a newly released "A" film with well-known movie stars who could fill a theater. Double features used to be popular with people who wanted to spend a full night at the movies.

But even if Reagan's acting partners were, like him, relatively unknown, he suddenly found himself hobnobbing with some of the biggest film stars in the world—people like Humphrey Bogart, Errol Flynn, Olivia de Havilland, Cary Grant, and Jimmy Cagney.

He also got to keep riding horses. The Army had transferred his duty post as a reserve officer to a military installation near Los Angeles, so he could still ride cavalry horses during monthly training.

In 1939, on the set of a comedy called *Brother Rat* about VMI, a men's military college, Reagan met another up-and-coming actor named Jane Wyman. She was a smart, pretty brunette with sparkling blue eyes, a good sense of humor, and a Catholic upbringing. The two fell in love, and their romance was featured in the newspapers by the famous gossip columnist Louella Parsons as a kind of Hollywood dream-come-true. They were married and soon had a daughter, Maureen, and not long after that adopted a son, Michael.

Meantime, Reagan was becoming an important player at Warner Brothers. Almost from the moment he got there, he had been trying to interest someone in making a film about the famous Notre Dame coach Knute Rockne, who had been killed in a plane crash a few years earlier. Especially poignant to the movie Reagan envisioned was the story of George Gipp—"the Gipper"—one of Rockne's most famous halfbacks, who died two weeks after his last game, on his deathbed famously urging Rockne to tell the team to go out and "win one for the Gipper."

Around the Warner's lot, Reagan would buttonhole anyone he thought had any chance to help get the movie made, letting them know that he could write the screenplay—already had one in his head in fact. And then one day he picked up a copy of *Variety*, the industry trade magazine, and was horrified to read that Warner's was already in casting to do his movie, with Pat O'Brien in the role of Rockne.

When he complained, one of the studio's leading producers, who was also a friend, told him, "You talk too much." It was the old Hollywood story of people shamelessly stealing other people's ideas.

Nevertheless, Reagan rushed over to see the man who was making the movie, only to be told he didn't fit the part. "Gipp was one of the greatest football players of all time," the producer calmly informed Reagan. Astonished, Reagan stormed out of the office and raced home to collect pictures of himself from his football days at Eureka. He returned to the studio and slammed them down on the producer's desk without a word.

The producer studied them for a moment, then asked if Reagan would leave them with him. Reagan had hardly gotten through the door of his house when the phone rang. It was casting. At 8:00 next morning, he was shooting a screen test for the part of George Gipp—his first A picture.

Knute Rockne, All American was, of course, a smash hit, and it put Reagan where he had wanted and worked so hard to be. Even when he'd made the varsity football teams at Dixon High and Eureka, he was never satisfied until he made first string. Immediately he was cast as one of the two leading men in another A picture, a Civil War era cavalry epic with Errol Flynn called *Santa Fe Trail*.

Here were the beginnings of Reagan's long experience with scene-stealing, the time-honored contrivance by some actors to upstage their counterparts, so as to focus all attention upon themselves. Flynn was one of the worst offenders.

They were shooting in the middle of the night around a campfire, when Flynn suddenly went to the director for a private conference. When it was over, Reagan was told to move back behind two very tall actor-soldiers, which would have left his single line in the scene dangling in the air with his face mostly hidden, while Flynn remained in the spotlight.

Reagan soon realized this, and while they began to rehearse the shot, he scraped up a little mound of dirt with his boots. He kept piling it up until it was about six inches high, and when it was time to do the scene, he stepped up on it, making himself about 6'10". When it came time for him to deliver his line, much to Flynn's dismay, Reagan towered above the tall extras in front of him.

Reagan's next movie was *The Bad Man*, with the great old actor Lionel Barrymore, another notorious upstager, who was by then confined to his famous wheelchair. He would steal scenes by suddenly wheeling himself off while delivering his lines, effectively cutting his opposing actor out of the shot. Several times Barrymore even ran over Reagan's toes with his chair.

But the most notorious upstager in all of Hollywood was the actor Wallace Beery, who was said to steal scenes even in close-ups, as Reagan had been warned by the director. But as he began delivering his lines while holding a horse, Reagan was not prepared to find that Beery had somehow maneuvered himself around to get his full face to the camera—when he was supposed to be standing on the other side of the horse!

Reagan admired and liked all these actors, who were among the most famous of their era, but he was also learning harsh lessons about how picture-making works at its highest level. It is probably similar to a talented college football player entering the pros and finding out some of the tricks the veterans use. Except that in football you're supposed to use them against an opposing team—not people you're trying to make a movie with!

★ ★ ★

In the meantime, Reagan decided he was making enough money to bring his parents west, and to buy them the house they had never been able to afford. His father had a heart condition, which had worsened to the point where he couldn't keep to the rigors of a full time job, but he was still a proud man who might feel self-conscious taking something that looked like charity. So Reagan came up with an inspired solution.

By now he was receiving huge amounts of fan mail, and he arranged for his father to become his secretary, certified to drive to the Warner's lot every day and pick up all this mail with its various requests for photographs and autographs, and answer it from the comfort of his and Nelle Reagan's new home. It was the perfect answer, and his father handled this duty admirably until his death a few years later at the age of fifty-eight.

Before he died, however, Reagan's father quit drinking for good and became a faithful churchgoer. The happiest moment in his life, he confided to Nelle Reagan, was when Dutch invited him to the grand opening of *Knute Rockne, All American*, which was held at Notre Dame in

South Bend, Indiana. Not only was the cast present, but other big stars as well, such as Bob Hope.

"I was there," he said to Nelle right before he died, "when our son became a star."

Reagan's mother lived on another twenty-one years, still on her mission helping out the less fortunate, until she passed away in 1964 of an ailment diagnosed then as "dementia" or "hardening of the arteries." We know it now as Alzheimer's Disease.

★ ★ ★

Reagan had been making movies for four years when, in 1941, stardom finally found him. He had graduated from B movies to A movies, but always as a leading man, not a star. His performance in *Kings Row* changed all of that.

A dark, sprawling melodrama set in a small town, *Kings Row*, based on the novel by Henry Bellamann, featured an all-star cast including Charles Coburn, Claude Rains, Ann Sheridan, and Robert Cummings. At one point the character played by Reagan has his legs unnecessarily amputated by a sadistic doctor seeking revenge for his daughter.

This was to prove the most memorable scene, with the most memorable line, largely because Reagan, deliberately or not, engaged in a form of "method acting" before it was shot. The scene is set in a hospital room as Reagan's character comes out of his anesthetic and realizes to his great horror that his legs have been amputated at the knees. Reagan worried about how to play the scene for days, but when he arrived on the set and saw that they had cut a hole in the mattress of his hospital bed, he climbed in and pulled the sheet over him.

Looking at himself, with his legs dangling down through the hole, he began to imagine what it would be like to be legless. A chill rose in him as he entered more into the scene, feeling that he actually *was* legless. He stayed there purposely for nearly an hour, letting his mind run wild with how he might feel, and when the director arrived, he whispered to him, "No rehearsal—just shoot it."

As the camera pans in on his legless form under the hospital sheet, he slowly becomes aware something is wrong, and looks down, first in fear, then in shock, and finally in horror, before screaming to his wife, "Randy, where is the rest of me!"

The director, Sam Wood, nodded and said, "Print it." There was no need for a retake.

The way he delivered that line alone propelled Reagan to stardom, but alas, it was short-lived.

★ ★ ★

Kings Row was nominated for three academy awards that year, but faced stiff competition. Reagan's own studio, for instance, had released the fabulous *Yankee Doodle Dandy*, starring Jimmy Cagney, but even that wasn't enough to beat out the touching story of *Mrs. Miniver*, about an English family during World War II.

The war came to the United States on December 7, 1941, when the Japanese attacked the U.S. Naval Base at Pearl Harbor. By then Reagan had finished shooting *Kings Row* for Warner Brothers, but the United States Army was just getting started with him. Not long afterward, Lieutenant Ronald Reagan received notice from the War Department that he was now on active duty. They gave him two weeks to get his affairs in order.

CHAPTER SIX

LIEUTENANT REAGAN, U.S. ARMY

Several years earlier, when Reagan had passed his first Army physical exam, he had managed to cheat on his eyesight test. He did it because you had to have near perfect sight to join the cavalry, and without his glasses he was legally blind.

But as he tells it, there is an old trick somebody had taught him, which is that if you are nearsighted, you can gain almost perfect vision by looking through a pinhole. Of course you can't go through life looking through pinholes, but it was enough to get him past the eye exam. They had told him to hold his hand over one eye when he read the eye chart, and he did, but squeezed his fingers apart just a hair, as if he were looking through a pinhole, and managed to read the chart not with the uncovered eye, but with the one he had his hand to. It worked with the other eye too, and he was able to pass his physical.

No such luck, however, when he reported to Fort Mason in San Francisco for his new physical. One of the examining doctors remarked that if they sent him oversees with that kind of eyesight, "You'd shoot a general." The other said, "Yes, and you'd miss him."

With that, they marked Reagan fit for duty only in the continental U.S., and set him to work as a liaison officer to the Navy. His job was loading convoys bound for Australia, from which Washington hoped to build up a large force to attack the Japanese in the South Pacific.

It was dull, routine business, but that didn't last long either. The U.S. Army Air Corps, it seemed, was building a motion picture intelligence unit to produce combat training films and documentaries, and because of his movie experience, Reagan was tapped for duty with it.

The unit set up in the Culver City studios of Hal Roach—who became famous for making *The Little Rascals* comedy shorts—and promptly dubbed it "Fort Roach." Reagan was the group's administrative officer, or adjutant, and his first duty was to recruit movie people—directors, artists, cameramen, film cutters, technicians, grips, and gaffers—thirteen hundred of them in all—and soon they were sending cameramen to all parts of the globe where the Army Air Corps was operating. Rough footage was expedited back to "Fort Roach" and used for training films for young fliers. At one point the outfit made a training film for aerial gunners that actually cut their training course by six weeks.

One of their projects was so secret its existence remained practically unknown until Reagan wrote about it in his 1965 autobiography, *Where's the Rest of Me?*. It involved nothing less than a reconstruction of the entire city of Tokyo.

As Reagan explained, most of the briefings given to bomber pilots consisted of an officer on a stage with a pointing stick and a series of large maps on easels. But the creative juices in Reagan's Hollywood-heavy film unit began flowing, and they decided there was a better way.

First they collected pictures of Tokyo and other important Japanese cities—old film, new film, photographs brought in by former missionaries or one-time tourists—and using all of this information, plus the most current maps, they began to build an enormous replica of the

Japanese capital in miniature. Then, by mounting a camera on a moving crane, they filmed their stage-prop Tokyo from practically every angle, altitude, and approach imaginable. Reagan narrated the film himself.

At first the Air Force brass were skeptical, but when they saw the finished product they were astonished, and threw a cloak of secrecy over the whole place, including a 24-hour guard. The filmmakers had managed to furnish pilots with the actual "feeling" of flying over Tokyo, with important landmarks they could use as guides. In those days, well before our GPS and other location systems were available, this was a godsend. Reagan narrated the film and remained justly proud of it: "Only an outfit like ours could have accomplished this task. Here was the true magic of motion picture making, the climax of years of miracle-working that had made Hollywood the film capital of the world."

★ ★ ★

In the last year of the war, Washington issued a ruling that jolted Reagan in much the same way the arrival of the government's welfare bureaucrats did in Dixon years before, as they undermined his father's work program during the Great Depression.

Somebody in Washington, it seems, had decided that civilian workers at military posts throughout the country would be reduced by 35 percent and replaced by government Civil Service employees. As post adjutant, Reagan soon began to hear complaints that many of these Civil Service people were incompetent, but it made little difference.

The Civil Service people who arrived at Fort Roach began bossing the military people around, Reagan included. Soon they had organized a giant bureaucracy with floor-to-ceiling files, and the regulations they brought with them made it virtually impossible to discharge anyone for incompetence. It was Reagan's first inkling that a bureaucracy, once it is established, tends to perpetuate itself into the eternal forever.

Still, he remained a staunch liberal and supporter of Roosevelt's New Deal policies. He wasn't ready yet for his great conversion. But other events would soon see to that.

★ ★ ★

Throughout Reagan's youth, sports and acting had been two of his greatest avocations, and along the way he had added a third, horseback riding. Yet there was another calling that even he never realized had buried itself deeply in his psyche, and that was politics. At Dixon High, he'd been president of the student body. At Eureka College, as a freshman, he'd been sought out to lead a student strike against what most everybody thought were unfair policies. And he'd won it.

Despite the demands of keeping his grades up, playing football, and acting in plays, he'd still managed to find time to keep his hand in campus politics. First as a member of the Eureka student senate, then as the school's student body president, Reagan always made a point of asserting himself as a political leader. Now he was about to do it again, but not in the arena of normal politics; instead he was poised to enter what was possibly the most vicious political snake pit of all—the politics of labor unions.

True to his upbringing as a Democrat, Reagan had always been a committed believer in labor unions, but when he got to Hollywood it wouldn't have mattered if he weren't. The movie unions were "closed shop," meaning that everyone had to join or they were not allowed to work. There were unions for everything and everybody, except the producers, who were considered "management." All jobs were covered, from acting to set designing, to paper-hanging, electrical work, cartoonists, story readers, carpentry, camera operation, projectionists, stagehands, machinists, film cutting, furniture moving, painting, makeup, tailoring, hair-styling—forty-three unions in all.

At first, even though he was a union man in theory, Reagan balked at the notion of joining a union himself. Unions were fine for laboring people, but he considered actors to be "artists," and therefore somehow above such common organizations. Besides, as he noted afterward, "I was doing all right for myself; a union seemed unnecessary."

Accordingly, one day in the Warner's commissary he let his feelings be known, and immediately was taken aside by the prominent actress Helen Broderick, who set him straight. The Screen Actors Guild—or SAG—she informed him, was almost a sacred institution in the movie business. Prior to its formation in 1933, producers regularly took advantage of lesser actors, requiring them to work long hours, sometimes under arduous conditions, often without proper meal breaks, and the pay was usually low and frequently arbitrary. In short, until they unionized, most of the actors were treated like trash.

For four years the producers—"management"—refused to negotiate with SAG and tried to break it up, blacklisting known members and hiring detectives to find out who else belonged. Finally, in 1937, the year Reagan got to Hollywood, some 5,000 actors voted to go on strike, which prompted the movie studios to recognize SAG and negotiate a contract with it.

After this dressing down by Helen Broderick, Reagan went to the SAG office and filled out his union application, and the following year he was elected as a board member, a position he accepted, "with awe and pleasure."

As he pointed out later, the people who made SAG work were the ones "who really didn't need it"—the big movie stars of the day such as James Cagney, Humphrey Bogart, the Marx Brothers, Robert Montgomery, Cary Grant, Dick Powell, and scores of others who made huge salaries and were never in need of work. The studios might have blacklisted the bit-players and B-movie actors, but they certainly couldn't blacklist their stars, or they'd be out of business.

When Reagan returned from the Army at the close of the war, he was immediately re-appointed to SAG's board of directors and stepped straight into the ugliest strike in the history of Hollywood.

It started over a nasty and long-simmering jurisdictional dispute between two craft unions, but quickly engulfed the entire business. As a matter of labor theory, when one union goes out on strike, the others are bound to follow and not cross the picket lines of the striking union. But in this case, the parent organization of all Hollywood unions, the powerful American Federation of Labor, or AFL, disavowed the strike and told everyone to go back to work.

The striking union ignored this and continued to picket, leaving the other unions in a quandary. Some voted to back the strikers, others voted to obey the edict of the AFL. Name-calling and threats began to characterize the dispute. Eventually violence broke out; cars were overturned by enraged strikers, and there were beatings and rioting as well.

SAG had become the critical player in the strike, since the studios could hire strikebreakers to perform most tasks (though not acting—nobody would pay to see a Cary Grant movie without Cary Grant).

Reagan offered to host a meeting between the studio heads and the striking union to find out "what was going on." At the meeting, he soon concluded that the striking union wasn't trying to improve the working conditions or get more money for its members, but rather to absorb a smaller union into its own. In other words, the strike was a "phony."

He called for a meeting of the full SAG membership to vote on whether or not to cross the picket lines. Several days before the meeting, he received an anonymous phone call while on a movie set. The caller threatened Reagan with violence if he held the SAG meeting, telling him, "Your face will never be in pictures again." He later was told that the plot was to throw disfiguring acid in his face.

When he got back to the studio offices, the police were there. They gave him a pistol and a shoulder holster and put an armed guard on his house twenty-four hours a day. He held the meeting anyway, and the SAG members voted overwhelmingly to cross the picket lines. He would carry the pistol for six months.

After this, the strike got even nastier, and it confronted Reagan with a challenge he had only dimly suspected existed until now: that Communists with ties to the Soviet Union were attempting to infiltrate the Hollywood unions, in order to influence the content of movies to reflect their political point of view.

★ ★ ★

It must be remembered that, by 1946, the United States and the rest of what was called the Free World were already becoming locked in the Cold War with the powerful Soviet Union. Immediately after the Second World War ended, Soviet Russia had established all across Europe what Britain's Prime Minister Winston Churchill labeled the Iron Curtain, a chain of Communist dictatorships in Eastern European countries that stretched across the continent from the North Sea to the Mediterranean.

During the war the Soviets (previously allied with Adolf Hitler) joined the Allies in the fight against Nazi Germany. But no sooner had peace been restored than the Soviets began taking over the countries Hitler had formerly occupied. They set up Communist "puppet" regimes throughout most of Eastern Europe, including Poland, Austria, Hungary, Czechoslovakia, half of Germany, the Baltic States, and others. At the same time, Soviet agents were operating in most of the rest of Europe, in an attempt to turn those countries Communist as well.

Likewise, the Soviets were working frantically to build their own atomic bomb to threaten the United States and Western Europe. (They finally succeeded in doing so in 1949, after stealing atomic secrets from the U.S. and Great Britain through Communist spies, some of whom, it is sad to say, were American and British citizens.)

Russia had been the world's first country to fall to Communism. This occurred in a bloody revolution in 1917, as the First World War raged in Europe. The Communist leaders realized that their political and economic system would not work properly unless the rest of the world could be converted to Communism too, either peaceably or by force. To achieve this, they created an organization, the Communist *Internationale* or Comintern, with representatives from all countries, whose job was to infiltrate non-Communist governments and steer them toward the political dictatorship of the Soviet Union.

Early on, long before the Cold War began, Soviet propaganda operatives understood that control of the news media and performing arts of a nation would go a long way toward convincing that nation's people that Communism was a superior way of life. Their first efforts at recruiting American performing artists for Communism began in the 1920s and continued through the 1930s. Many of their recruits were stage actors, writers, and directors who had gone to study at the famous Moscow Theater, which was run by the Soviet state. Once there, the conversion process was begun.

When these people returned to the U.S., many of them joined the radical Group Theater in New York City, and the plays they produced often espoused Communist themes.

Then, as movies became more and more popular, many of these same artists moved west to Hollywood, which soon became known as the Motion Picture Capital of the World. They carried their Communist ideas with them.

At the same time, Communists were employing themselves in a mighty effort to infiltrate American labor unions with the notion of starting a revolution "from the bottom up." These included teachers' unions, newspaper unions, and of course, Hollywood movie unions.

★ ★ ★

Such was the situation that Reagan confronted as the leader of the Screen Actors Guild during the Hollywood union strike. The head of the striking union was pro-Communist, and after the actors voted to cross his picket lines and go to work, he took drastic measures. He contacted the head of the longshoremen's union in San Francisco, who was a Communist named Harry Bridges, and requested help.

Bridges was only too happy to comply, sending down a number of thugs to provoke violence at the Hollywood studios. This they hoped would create the beginnings of a "class struggle" between rich and poor, a guiding principle of Communist takeovers.

The San Francisco thugs performed their job as advertised. The studios had arranged for buses to carry actors across the picket lines. Thugs stoned the buses, threw hot coffee in the faces of others who tried to cross, and strewed nails and tacks in the path of movie stars' automobiles. They wielded clubs and beat other non-striking workers who tried to cross, turned over numerous cars, and burned others. Some people were knifed. It was a classic case of union intimidation.

Seven movie studios were temporarily shut down before police could restore order, and a dozen or more people were taken to the hospital. In the end the striking union was forced to back down by the other movie unions, but the affair had a profound effect on the political education of Ronald Reagan.

CHAPTER SEVEN

THE POLITICAL CONVERSION OF RONALD REAGAN

As we have seen, Reagan was raised a Democrat in the liberal tradition. He idolized Franklin Roosevelt, who had been elected the year he graduated from college. "Republican" was a dirty word around the Reagan household, as they held with the general belief that Republicans were the "party of the rich," the party of "big business."

How could this have happened to the "party of Lincoln," which had been founded less than eighty years earlier as a liberal-leaning, anti-slavery movement? It is an interesting question to explore.

Before the Civil War, many wealthy northerners were opposed to slavery and joined the Republicans in ridding the country of it, ultimately by force of arms. But after that was accomplished, most remained committed Republicans, while many of those in the "lower classes"—the Irish and other immigrant groups who were clustered in big cities—had come under the sway of Democratic political machines.

During the latter part of the nineteenth century and early part of the twentieth, the Republicans began to advertise themselves as conservatives and supporters and promoters of business. As one Republican president famously put it: "The business of America is business."*

Until the stock market crash of 1929 and the ensuing Great Depression, the country had been mostly prosperous, and the Republicans took credit for it. Democrats, on the other hand, had begun to bill themselves as the party of "the little man," which attracted social liberals into their ranks. These included women's suffrage advocates, labor union members, and, as the Depression progressed, people who wanted the government to provide them with more assistance.

But also, beginning after the First World War, there was a small but dedicated class of Americans who had begun to question the very theory of capitalism, under which our economic system operates. Many of these people embraced socialism as defined by the political philosophers Karl Marx and Friedrich Engels in 1867. Marx and Engels had described a new system under which the government itself would own all major utilities, banks, manufactories, and large agricultural holdings, and control the money supply. The government would set the people to working in jobs it decided would be most useful to the state, and dispense goods and services to them according to need.

Under this system there would be no religion; the "state" would be all things to all men, as defined by Marx's famous declaration that his "object in life is to dethrone God and destroy capitalism."

The liberals were for the most part sincere, good-hearted citizens who were appalled at the plight of Northern big-city slum-dwellers or impoverished Southern sharecroppers. They believed that a large, strong central government could run things better, plan things better, and improve working and living conditions for the downtrodden.

---

* Calvin Coolidge, "The Press Under a Free Government," speech given before the American Society of Newspaper Editors, January 17, 1925. His actual words were, "The business of the American people is business," but the phrase is more commonly quoted this way.

Furthermore, many of them thought there was much to admire in the Communist system of Soviet Russia. The news stories coming out of the Soviet Union were mostly glowing reports of the successes of Communism: pictures of happy peasants harvesting crops or working on immense public works projects.

What the world was not shown, however, was the dark, horrible side of Communism in which the Soviet dictator at that time, Joseph Stalin, was deliberately starving to death millions of his own people, executing thousands of others, and banishing hundreds of thousands more to the gulags of Siberia and other awful places.

Without knowledge of this, however (or choosing not to believe it), certain of the intellectual class of Democrats considered it fashionable or "chic" to identify with Soviet Communism. Vladimir Lenin, a founder of Russian Communism, once described such people as "useful idiots." Many of the artistically inclined gravitated toward this view, and Hollywood was no exception.

One of those exceptions, however, was Ronald Reagan. He was, by his own later admission, almost pitifully naïve, and was about to find out just how naïve he was. In college he had thrown himself into football, swimming, student politics, and studies, managing to graduate with the proverbial "gentleman's C." As a sportscaster he concentrated on sports. When he became an actor, he committed his life to acting, and when the Army called him up, he devoted himself to his military duties.

When Reagan arrived in Hollywood, he was aware that there were people there with leftist, socialist, even Communist leanings, but he assumed they were merely ultra-liberals. He did not realize that some of these people were actual American Communists, who had rejected their loyalty to the United States and instead pledged it to the Soviet Union. They were dedicated to the ultimate overthrow of the federal government in Washington.

To actually become Communists, these people had to undergo a lengthy process of re-education and indoctrination, concluding with a pledge of allegiance to the Soviet system. Once confirmed as Communists, their role in the party was essentially threefold: to act as agents pushing the Soviet cause in the United States, to perform spying duties when ordered, and to foment revolution or "class struggle" among the American people.

Though there were few such hardcore Communists in the U.S., they still managed to cause a lot of trouble. A number were embedded in the government itself, some, unfortunately, in top-secret positions. Others had infiltrated the labor unions, and some were in academia. And they managed to attract many "fellow travelers," or "Pinkos" as they were called. True Communists were known as "Reds." The "fellow travelers" were the "radicals," or "ultra-liberals," and many of them were employed in the motion picture industry, including some well-known movie stars of the era.

There weren't many actual Communists among the movie stars, but the "fellow travelers" often donated money, made public appearances, or lent their names to causes promoted by the Communists. Most of Hollywood's true Communists were screenplay writers and a few directors.

John Garfield, a famous actor Reagan knew and liked, later admitted to the FBI that he had been duped by the Communists. Reagan once attended a meeting with Garfield, where he found himself being shouted down by Communists when he tried to speak. Garfield stood up and said, "Why don't you let him talk?" As Reagan continued his speech, he saw Garfield suddenly seized in the rear of the crowd by the Communist actor Howard Da Silva, who grabbed him by his shirtfront and began upbraiding him for his impertinence.

Sterling Hayden, another movie star who had recently quit the Communist Party, told a congressional committee investigating Soviet infiltration of Hollywood unions that Reagan had been a "one-man battalion" preventing a Communist takeover of Hollywood.

So what exactly did Reagan do? He stood up to the Communists at a time when it was very unpopular among many of his associates to do so.

An organization of nearly a thousand movie elite had been formed to promote liberal causes. It was called Hollywood Independent Citizens Committee of the Arts, Sciences, and Professions (known in short as HICCASP). It sounded like a good cause to Reagan, so he joined it too, and soon found himself on its board of directors.

At his first board meeting, Reagan was astonished to find more than seventy people in attendance, including many he knew to be dedicated leftists. Seventy people was a remarkably large number for a board of directors. Reagan sat next to Dore Schary, the powerful head of MGM, and wondered aloud to him why all those people were there.

"Stick around," was Schary's strange reply.

Soon James "Jimmy" Roosevelt (the U.S. president's son) stood up and told the group that some members had expressed suspicions that HICCASP was somehow being turned into a Communist front organization. He asked the board to issue a public proclamation to repudiate Communism. Immediately, the assembly broke into a furious uproar.

Roosevelt's remarks were intended as a ruse to "smoke out" Communists from the organization. They were precipitated by an incident from the previous month involving *Gone with the Wind* star Olivia de Havilland. De Havilland had been asked to give a speech, written by the acclaimed screenwriter Dalton Trumbo, at a Seattle rally for HICCASP. Trumbo, it was later revealed, was a Communist Party member.

Trumbo's speech alarmed de Havilland, because it condemned the administration in Washington for trying to start a war with Soviet Russia and contained other, similar propaganda. When she showed Trumbo's speech to Jimmy Roosevelt, he and others rewrote it to say that, contrary to rumors, HICCASP was not a Communist organization, but that Communists had "driven a wedge" into the liberal group.

Trumbo, of course was furious, and the meeting Reagan attended that July night in 1946 was meant to "clear the air," which it certainly did not.

No sooner had Roosevelt demanded that HICCASP publicly renounce Communism than Trumbo rose up vowing that he would fight for Russia if war broke out between the U.S. and the Soviets. Next a famous bandleader jumped to his feet, hollering that he could recite the entire Soviet constitution from memory, and that "it was a lot more democratic than that of the United States."

Reagan stood up and echoed what Roosevelt had said, wondering why so many board members were against repudiating Communism. He was greeted with a chorus of vituperation, people shouting that he was a "fascist," a "witch hunter," "capitalist scum," and "an enemy of the proletariat."

Pandemonium broke out, with people yelling and banging their fists on tables. Some had to be removed from the room, and one woman suffered a heart attack and was taken to the hospital.

Reagan hastily scribbled down a "statement of policy" on the back of an envelope, which said: "We reaffirm our belief in free enterprise and the democratic system and repudiate Communism as desirable for the United States."

At this, a prominent screenwriter named Howard W. Lawson began shaking his finger under Reagan's nose and screaming, "This organization will never adopt a statement which endorses free enterprise and repudiates Communism!" He further declared, "For your information, I may add that a two-party system is in no way necessary, or even desirable, for a democracy!"

Reagan responded, reasonably enough, that the entire membership of HICCASP should be allowed to decide, by secret ballot, whether or not they approved of the policy statement.

At this, Lawson revealed the elitism embedded in Communist dogma: "The membership," he informed Reagan, "isn't politically sophisticated enough to make this decision."

In the end the HICCASP "executive committee" rejected Reagan's proposal, and it became apparent to everyone that Communists had seriously infiltrated the organization. Reagan, de Havilland, Roosevelt, and a host of other prominent members resigned, which of course spelled the end of HICCASP, since stars like these had made it what it was in the first place.

But the incident also became an epiphany for Ronald Reagan, one of those critical realizations that changes one's life forever. He was beginning to believe that, whether they were "card-carrying" Communists or not, the liberals—the ultra-liberals, "fellow travelers" of the Communists—were deliberately acting against the best interests of the United States.

★ ★ ★

In the meantime, various government entities were investigating reports that Communists were trying to take over Hollywood unions. One was a committee of the California State Senate, which held hearings and reported that HICCASP was indeed a Communist front organization.

Another was the U.S. Congress's House Un-American Activities Committee (HUAC), which opened a series of hearings that soon became widely controversial. The committee began calling members of the Hollywood community as witnesses—actors, directors, and screenwriters.

Some of these people actually were Communists. A number of them read opening statements that were highly critical of the committee, then refused to answer questions about whether or not they were Communists, citing the Constitution's Fifth Amendment guarantee against self-incrimination. This was merely a ploy, since being a Communist was not a crime in the United States.

A group of movie stars who were not in fact Communists, but who either resented being asked questions before the committee—or resented their friends being asked questions—held public demonstrations in which they denounced HUAC.

This did not go over particularly well with most American people, since they had grown uneasy over the Soviet Union's behavior in Europe, and its spying and warlike stance against the United States.

★ ★ ★

After the Communist takeover of Russia in 1917, and all through the 1920s and '30s, most Americans had viewed the Communists with suspicion but not alarm, since they seemed to pose no particular threat to the United States. But when the Soviet Union emerged from World War II as an immensely powerful, well-armed, and hostile force, the West was, to say the least, disturbed.

Nevertheless, HUAC began to step over its bounds by abusing some of the so-called "unfriendly" witnesses (those who took the Fifth Amendment). Slurs were made against them, and when Hollywood box office sales began to reflect public dissatisfaction with leftists and Communists in the movie industry, the heads of the studios reacted. They issued a decree called the Waldorf Statement (named after the New York City hotel in which they were meeting), promising that henceforth they would not employ anyone known to be a Communist, or who refused to answer questions under oath about whether or not they were Communists. This was the famous "blacklist."

The original blacklist consisted only of ten screenwriters who had pleaded the Fifth Amendment before HUAC, but was expanded over the months and years to include several hundred Hollywood employees.

Reagan, like many other well-known Hollywood stars, had testified before HUAC as a "friendly" witness, meaning that he told the committee what he knew, including, in private testimony, giving the names of those he knew or suspected as being Communist. But he also told the committee that the notion of outlawing the Communist Party was probably a bad idea. "We have spent one hundred seventy years in this country on the basis that democracy is strong enough to stand up and fight against the inroads of any ideology," he said.

He explained that he and others had used democracy to fight and contain the Communists in SAG. The best way to beat Communism, he added, was "to make democracy work." He told the committee that under his leadership at SAG they "exposed the [Communists'] lies when we came across them," and stopped them from "trying to run a majority of the organization with a well-organized minority."

Reagan was also undergoing an intellectual realization. He now thoroughly understood that Communists had infiltrated almost every nook and cranny of the Hollywood unions—and further that their interests and goals were directly opposed to everything that he believed America stood for.

"Now I knew from firsthand experience," he said, "how Communists used lies, deceit, violence, or any other tactic that suited them to advance the cause of Soviet expansionism."

On the other hand, he was now president of the Screen Actors Guild and found himself representing members accused of being Communists when in fact they were not. These included some big stars such as Jimmy Cagney, Humphrey Bogart, Edward G. Robinson, and a number of lesser actors, whose mere "association" with Communists or known Communist causes was threatening their reputations, and in some cases their livelihood.

Reagan, Olivia de Havilland, and others formed an "industry council" to help these people clear their names, both with the public and the studio heads who threatened to blacklist them. Reagan arranged for anyone who denied being a Communist to voluntarily speak with the FBI, or even with HUAC, and his council would vouch for his or her innocence.

It worked. In the end, Reagan's council cleared scores of people who were wrongly accused of being Communists.

CHAPTER EIGHT

A REVERSAL OF FORTUNES

So far, Ronald Reagan seemed to have led a charmed life. Even though he'd been raised in relative poverty, he never let it bother him; he was popular as an athlete and leader in both high school and college. He'd landed an important sportscasting job in the middle of the Great Depression, until even greater fortune smiled upon him after his trip to Hollywood. He was now a famous movie star with a fabulous salary, had broken Communist attempts to infiltrate his union, and successfully defended the majority of his fellow actors during the HUAC hearings in Washington. He was thirty-seven years old, with a beautiful wife and two lovely children. The world was his oyster—but beginning in 1948, it came close to falling apart.

First, as soon as Reagan returned from testifying in Washington, his wife, Jane Wyman, told him she wanted a divorce. It was rumored that she had grown tired of all his talk of politics, and the union, and Communism. Years afterward she would say, "I don't know a damn thing about politics." While Reagan was so deeply involved in political matters, she had just won an Academy Award as best actress, and now was, if anything, even more famous than he was.

Reagan was stunned and shattered. He wrote afterward that there probably had been warning signs, but he'd been too busy to see them, adding, "Small-town boys grow up thinking that only other people get divorced."

He moved into an apartment and tried to reshape his life, but remained distraught over the failure of the marriage and what he knew must be the hurt to his children, seven-year-old Maureen and three-year-old Michael. After a while, he began dating around, and it was widely reported in the gossip columns that he was seen with some of the most glamorous actresses of the day—Lana Turner, Rita Hayworth, and others.

That same year, 1948, he went to England to make *The Hasty Heart*, one of his best movies, and was struck by how depressed and unmanageable that country had become under the Labor-Socialist government. He found the infamous London smog abominable, the lack of heating uncomfortable, and the food strange and unpalatable. But he made good friends with the cast, saw Ireland, the country of his ancestors, and visited Wales too.

After film shooting ended, he had eight days before his ship sailed, so he decided on a quick tour to the South of France. On the drive down he was riveted by the sight of burned-out German tanks still lying in farmers' fields three years after the war ended, and saddened by temporary graves of soldiers along the roadside, marked by white crosses with helmets resting on top. In Monte Carlo, on the French Riviera, he gambled the nights away in the casinos, "winning wads and wads of paper francs, which turned out to be worth about sixty-five dollars when translated into real money."

All in all, his first trip abroad proved an interesting experience, but still he was lonely. As with the loss of Margaret Cleaver, his high school and college sweetheart, he wrote, "My loneliness was not from being unloved, but rather from not loving. Looking back, because at the time I wouldn't admit it to myself, I wanted to care for someone—yet I was building a sizable resistance to doing that very thing."

Upon returning to Hollywood, there was a more disturbing development: his movie career was in trouble.

★ ★ ★

Until 1948, the year of Reagan's divorce, Hollywood's seven large movie studios controlled, from beginning to end, all the elements of the moviemaking industry.

Each studio had its own actors, producers, screenwriters, and directors under contract. At Warner Brothers where Reagan worked, for example, a studio boss would tell a producer he could make this or that film. The producer would select one of the studio's directors to direct it, and one of its screenwriters to write it. The producer would then call Reagan or one of the other actors to star in it, along with the rest of the cast. The film would be developed, processed, and edited by the studio, which would then release it to the public through its own chain of movie theaters throughout the United States. Everybody was on studio salary. This was known as "The Studio System."

All that suddenly changed when the U.S. Department of Justice ruled that the studios were operating a monopoly, and persuaded the courts to force the studios to rid themselves of their theater chains. It was a major blow to the studios, because they would no longer be assured of recouping the costs of a movie by showing it in their own theaters, and it helped send the motion picture industry into a thirty-year slump. In turn, that caused the studios to abandon the contract system, which so many actors and others in the business had depended upon.

Reagan considered this an unwarranted government intrusion on an industry that produced 90 percent of all the movies ever made—

movies enjoyed by nearly 100 million people each week worldwide. Reagan later pointed out that someone like the epic moviemaker Cecil B. DeMille "can spend $13,000,000 making *The Ten Commandments*, and now if no theater owner wanted to show his picture, he was flatly forbidden from hiring a hall himself to show it."

At the same time, following a successful lawsuit by *Gone with the Wind* star Olivia de Havilland, a number of prominent movie actors released themselves from contracts with their particular studios and put their talents up for sale to the highest bidder. Reagan did this himself.

Also, many of the successful actors and actresses found themselves confronting the problem of what they felt was excessive taxation by the federal government. At that time, the highest income tax bracket was 94 percent, which was where Reagan found himself. This meant that after making a certain amount of money, Reagan could only keep six cents out of every dollar he earned. It was the same with the other major stars, and the result was that instead of making three or four or even five movies a year, the actors realized they only needed to make one, since 94 percent of every dollar they earned beyond that one picture would go to the federal government in taxes. Why bother?

Later, when he became president, Reagan would use this as an instructive explanation for his income tax reduction proposals. He pointed out that with so many stars refusing to make films, everyone was the worse for it. Thousands of workers who otherwise would have been employed in making the pictures had no jobs. The theater owners suffered a loss of attendance and revenue because there were fewer films to show. And the public was poorly served because the studios were less willing to take chances on higher quality movies, instead producing mostly tried, average-type films. It was a classic example of how high taxation was bad for America. When the government takes nearly all of a person's income for taxes, it eliminates the incentive to work, which in turn hurts many people at many different levels. That included the government itself, which received less tax revenue.

★ ★ ★

Before putting himself out as a free agent in the movie business, Reagan still had one film he was obligated to make for Warner Brothers, and he lived to regret it for the rest of his days. The film was called *That Hagen Girl* and was based on a smash-hit Broadway play. It was supposed to be the introduction to the movie-going public of Shirley Temple in a grownup role, after she had spent the past decade and a half as America's most beloved child actress. After reading the screenplay, Reagan tried to turn it down.

What he found particularly obnoxious was that the script called for Shirley Temple's character, a high school student, to fall in love with Reagan's, a teacher twice her age. Even in our own racy times, such a scenario would be hard for many audiences to digest.

When Jack Warner, head of the studio, more or less ordered him to make the picture, Reagan tried to get the director, an Englishman, to alter the script so that in the end Temple would fall for a boy her own age. But the director refused, telling Reagan, "I'm old enough to be my own wife's father."

Losing that argument, Reagan tried to get the director at least to drop one of the last lines in the movie where the Reagan character tells the teenage Shirley Temple, "I love you."

No dice.

After filming, Warner Brothers sneak-previewed the picture to an audience in Burbank, and Reagan sat in the back row, practically cringing. When he said to Shirley Temple on screen, "I love you," the audience erupted in a chorus of scandalized groans, "crying en masse 'Oh, no!'"

"I sat huddled in the darkness until I was sure the lobby would be empty," Reagan wrote. "You couldn't have got me to face that audience for a million bucks." He knew he shouldn't have made the movie.

Even though the studio cut the "I love you" line before releasing the picture to the general public, it was a flop anyway—which might, in some strange inadvertent way, have landed Ronald Reagan in the White House.

All his life, his mother had drilled into him the notion that things always work out for the best, even if they might not seem so at the time. It was, she always said, God's will.

So far, she'd been correct. Hadn't his loss of the job as manager of the sports department at Montgomery Ward—disappointing as it seemed at the time—turned out to be a blessing that led to his job as sportscaster, which in turn led to Hollywood?

But when *That Hagen Girl* came out, Dutch Reagan didn't see it as any kind of blessing in disguise.

★ ★ ★

Throughout his entire Hollywood career, he had wanted to make westerns. But—with a few notable exceptions—after his first big movie, *Santa Fe Trail*, all Warner Brothers seemed to want Reagan to do were drawing-room comedies.

But just before he'd left for England, he managed to persuade the studio to let him star in a western called *Ghost Mountain*, which he himself had suggested from a book he'd recently read. However, when his return ship from England docked in New York, Reagan picked up a copy of *Variety*, the show business newspaper, and was stunned to read that Warner's was making *Ghost Mountain* all right—but with Errol Flynn as the lead!

Not only that, but the studio was using the poor showing of *That Hagen Girl* as the excuse for replacing Reagan with Flynn in the picture!

Actors, and most especially stars, share a strange and intimate relationship with the movie-going public, far more so then than now.

People want the actor or actress they love to share their same values in the roles they play on the screen, as well as in real life. (Such was the temper of those times that in 1949, for example, the great movie star Ingrid Bergman was driven not only out of Hollywood, but out of the United States by an act of Congress, after she became pregnant by another man while still married to her husband.)

The public disapproval of the Reagan character's unseemly role in *That Hagen Girl* had transferred to Reagan himself. Put another way, many audiences somehow confuse the characters that actors play on the screen with the personal character of the actors themselves, which makes actors quite wary of the roles they choose to accept.

Besides, by the time Reagan returned from the war, he had not made a film in four years; theater audiences had moved on to other movie idols. Some big stars, such as Clark Gable and Jimmy Stewart, managed to overcome that wartime disadvantage, but Reagan had a more difficult time, especially since his work at SAG sometimes kept him from accepting good roles. And while it would not be fair to say the movie *That Hagen Girl* ruined his career, that movie—on top of all his other challenges—certainly didn't *help* it. Afterward, much of his on-screen work would be in television.

★ ★ ★

Meantime, as if getting tossed out of his house and watching his movie career go down the drain weren't enough, he broke his leg—and that is a mild way of putting it.

Finally free of his locked-in contract with Warner Brothers, Reagan was excited about doing a picture with the movie star Ida Lupino for Universal Pictures—a fast-paced crime drama that he hoped would get him out of the dog house from *That Hagen Girl*.

But the day before shooting was scheduled, Reagan had agreed to play in the annual Hollywood baseball game to benefit the City of Hope

Hospital. The charity draw was that the teams were made up of the movies' most famous comedians playing against the movies' most famous leading men. In the first inning, Reagan fell and managed to shatter his thighbone into six pieces.

It was an excruciating injury, and might have severely altered his performing career, had he not been cared for by excellent orthopedic surgeons who knew something about inserting steel rods into broken bones. But as it was, after the operation he spent two months in traction, lying flat in bed with his leg raised in a sling, months more on crutches in a cast, and then in a steel leg brace. Of course he was out of the picture with Ida Lupino.

When he had finally recuperated, Reagan again began to make pictures, but for the most part they were unmemorable—*Storm Warning, Louisa, The Last Outpost, She's Working Her Way Through College*, and—the one his critics and enemies gleefully pointed to as an example of his acting ability—*Bedtime For Bonzo*. This last was the story of a chimpanzee named Bonzo who was involved in a college professor's experiment to see what would happen if a chimpanzee were raised in a home just like a child. In fact it was a very funny comedy in which Reagan gave a credible performance as the college professor.

In his memoirs, Reagan delights in recalling the many occasions during filming in which the director, Fred De Cordova, would forget that Bonzo was actually an ape and start saying things like, "No Bonzo, in this scene you should…" and then slap himself on his head and cry, "What the hell am I doing?"

But in spite of these several trying years, a new sun was about to peek up over Reagan's horizon and guide him to places he'd never dreamed of going.

CHAPTER NINE

THE NEW SUN

One day Reagan took a phone call from the great film director and producer Mervyn LeRoy. At first he thought LeRoy was going to ask him to star in a film. As it turned out, what LeRoy had called about would become a far more important subject in Reagan's life.

LeRoy was calling Reagan in his capacity as president of SAG. A young actress named Nancy Davis had come to LeRoy concerned about her name, which was the same as that of another actress who was a leftist. Nancy was afraid her name would be confused and she'd be blacklisted. Could Reagan do anything to help?

Of course he could, Reagan said, and, after doing a check on her background, reported to LeRoy that everything with *his* Nancy Davis was fine, and that SAG would vouch for her if necessary.

However, that wasn't quite enough. Miss Davis wanted individual reassurance. LeRoy pleaded with Reagan to ask her to lunch or dinner and give her his personal support. Reagan thought about it for a moment, and the bachelor in him figured there wasn't much to lose; besides, "since she was on the contract list at MGM, she couldn't be repulsive."

He made the date, and on their way to the restaurant took up the question of her name being the same as the leftist girl's. He suggested the simplest solution was for her to go to the MGM publicity department and get herself a new name.

"But Nancy Davis is my name," she replied. This perked Reagan's interest. Here was a straight shooter.

That night they not only had dinner, but stayed out until 3:00 a.m. at a cabaret featuring the singer Sophie Tucker. Soon they became a couple, but it took Reagan two more years to pop the big question. One night he was in an SAG meeting and passed a note over to his good friend William Holden. "To hell with this! How would you like to be best man when I marry Nancy?"

Holden studied the note, then scribbled at the bottom, "It's about time."

They were married at the Little Brown Church in the San Fernando Valley. Holden was best man, and his wife, Ardis, made all the arrangements for a cake, photos, and so forth. It was a tiny wedding. Reagan had already been through a big one with Jane Wyman, and just saying the wedding vows was enough now. They honeymooned in Phoenix, where Nancy's parents had a vacation home. Her father—her stepfather actually, who had raised her—was an internationally known surgeon, and her mother had been a Broadway actress before her marriage.

In 1952, their daughter Patti was born, and six years later, a son, Ron. Over time the couple became inseparable; it was as if in many ways they were one and the same person. She stopped acting to raise the family, and soon found herself in carpools and PTA meetings with other Hollywood wives.

By 1960 they had bought a "dream house" in the Pacific Palisades overlooking the ocean. They also purchased a 350-acre ranch in the Santa Monica Mountains where Reagan could keep his horses. But Reagan was finding work harder to come by, now that he was a free agent. Under the old studio contract system, the work had been regular, even if some of the scripts were dogs. But as a freelancer, he soon found out that you are only as good as your last picture. It wasn't that Reagan didn't get any offers, it was just that most of the scripts were no good. To make things harder, Hollywood had gone into a slump, due in part to the breakup of the old Studio System, but mostly because of the recent explosion of the new medium of television.

★ ★ ★

It was believed in those days that television would be the kiss of death for Hollywood movie actors. "Nobody is going to pay money to see someone in pictures when they can see them on TV for free," or so the thinking went. But money was money, and Reagan found himself short of it. For a while he began accepting "guest" appearances on TV shows, which actually paid fairly well, and on one occasion he even did a stage act in Las Vegas, complete with straw hat and cane.

Then something came along that Reagan found too promising to turn down. Kiss of death or not, he accepted an offer to host, and occasionally star in, a new Sunday night television series called the *General Electric Theater*, sponsored by the General Electric Company. Each show would be a dramatized story, produced either in New York or Hollywood, sometimes on film, sometimes on live camera. It became an immediate smash hit and led the Sunday night ratings for eight years.

The work was regular and the pay was good; as part of the deal, the GE people also wanted Reagan to travel around the country making personal appearances at its 135 plants in 40 states. By his own account, Reagan met and shook hands with approximately 250,000 GE employees during his time on the show.

Not only that, but GE turned his home in the Pacific Palisades into "The House of the Future," completely electrifying it with all the latest GE gadgets, from dishwashers to toasters to an electric garbage disposal, which had just been invented. Sometimes Reagan hosted the *General Electric Theater* from his own kitchen.

For sixteen weeks a year, he would walk the assembly lines or laboratories in GE's 135 plants, meeting workers, signing autographs, and making impromptu speeches, sometimes from stages, but more often from atop tables or the backs of trucks. Sometimes he answered questions about how movie stunts were done, or makeup, but more often he gave speeches about Communism. In the beginning, he made it part of his personal mission to discredit the notion that most Hollywood people were Communists, but he saved his most persuasive arguments to describe the failed Communist takeover of the motion picture unions. This resonated with the GE employees more than anything else he said, Reagan remembered, because the vast majority were members of unions themselves, and they were aware of attempts at Communist infiltration.

In some of his speeches he attacked Communism itself, particularly the Soviet version, since it had become a direct threat to the democracies of the world. There have been various forms of Communism going back to the ancient Greeks, but the variety practiced in Reagan's day grew out of Karl Marx's writings in the mid-1800s. Marx was descended from a long line of Jewish rabbis, but was baptized a Christian to avoid religious persecution in his native Germany. Marx argued that industrialized European countries were largely divided into two opposing social classes: the "proletariat" (the masses of poor, exploited workers) and the "bourgeoisie" (rich factory owners and other big capitalists). In his vision, sometimes called "socialism," the proletariat throughout the entire world would rise up and overthrow the bourgeoisie and take charge of government. There would be no private property, or economy based on making money. In its place the government—or the "state"—would control everything, from wages paid to prices charged.

Marx famously wrote that the guiding principle of Communism would be: "From each according to his ability, to each according to his needs."

It sounds nice, until you consider that it would be the state that decided what your ability was, and what you needed. In other words, if the state decided that you should be a garbage man instead of a lawyer, then a garbage man you would be—and receive a garbage man's pay for it.

It was exactly the sort of thinking Reagan hated. He knew firsthand what an important thing it was to be able to rise up out of poverty and make something of yourself.

The form of Communism actually practiced—in the Soviet Union and its European satellites, as well as in China, Cuba, North Korea, and several countries in Southeast Asia—allowed only one political party. Dictators ran these nations, and their citizens enjoyed none of the freedoms granted under the U.S. Constitution—"freedom of speech," "freedom of religion," "freedom to assemble," freedom "to keep and bear arms," and the like. Or freedom to leave the country if you didn't like it, for that matter.

Reagan believed that people living under Communism lived as slaves.

★ ★ ★

As the years went by, his talks "underwent a kind of evolution, reflecting not only [his] changing philosophy," but also his newly confirmed opinion that the government in Washington was growing far too large, and intruding in negative ways on the everyday lives of citizens. Speaking from personal experience, Reagan pointed out the evils of high taxation. He described a U.S. government grown so big that it "owns and operates thousands of businesses tax-free, rent-free, and dividend-free—

in direct competition with private citizens, who must pay taxes to cover the losses incurred by these government-owned competitors." He believed America was headed toward socialism, just a step away from Communism. He never mentioned political parties or candidates or office-holders in these speeches, but his audiences got the picture.

Pretty soon, though, he would find out just how powerful the forces in Washington were.

It all began with his speaking out against TVA, a government project Reagan used to illustrate how government programs could grow beyond their original purpose. The TVA (or Tennessee Valley Authority) ran a huge electricity generating operation in the South. One day a bureaucrat in Washington went on the warpath over Reagan using the TVA as an example of improper big government programs. This person called the chairman of GE and informed him that the government wanted Reagan fired. Not only that, but he threatened if Reagan was not fired, the TVA might just cancel its $50 million worth of electric turbine contracts with GE.

To Reagan, this was the perfect case in point of how big government used its power to threaten and bully private citizens or companies. The chairman of GE thought so as well, and told the TVA man to take a hike.

Reagan's outspoken conservative views also attracted the attention of labor unions, which began circulating negative bulletins about him in their newsletters. When he arrived in St. Paul, Minnesota, to make a speech at a local high school, he discovered that the local teachers' union had passed a resolution demanding that he not be allowed to speak. He spoke anyway; a few days later he learned that the teachers' union was now demanding that the secretary of the U.S. Communist Party be invited to speak to the high school, on the grounds of giving the opposing view "equal time."

Big government remained Reagan's central theme on the road. He pointed to the federal farm programs, in which billions of taxpayer dollars are given to farmers *not* to grow certain crops. He was outraged to learn that the federal government "had six programs to help poultry growers increase egg production. It also had a seventh program costing almost as much as all the six others, to buy up surplus eggs."

He railed against welfare waste, fraud, and abuse, citing the example of welfare mothers not bothering to get married, because they would receive more financial benefits as single parents. He talked about a federal government job training program that cost the taxpayers 70 percent more than it would have cost to send each trainee to Harvard. And he had many other examples as well.

People began to notice, and not just the ones who disagreed with him. Reagan had become almost a one-man spokesman for conservative causes, and he remained a registered Democrat!

In 1962, Reagan worked on the gubernatorial campaign of Republican Richard Nixon in California, against Democrat governor Pat Brown. One day while he was making a speech, a woman in the audience stood up and interrupted him.

"Have you registered as a Republican yet?" she wanted to know.

Reagan, somewhat chagrined, replied that he hadn't.

"Well," she declared, "I am a registrar," and she marched down the aisle with a Republican registration card in one hand and a pen in the other, and handed them to Reagan.

He filled the card out. The audience cheered. His transformation was now complete.

Of it, he would later say, "I didn't leave the Democratic Party, the party left me."

★ ★ ★

One day in 1965, a group of influential California Republicans came to see Reagan at his home. Their question was, "Would you be willing to run for governor of the state?"

After his laughter had subsided, Reagan managed to ask them, "Are you out of your minds?"

Reagan had never given a thought to running for public office. As he put it in his memoirs, "After doing as much research as I had on the operations of government, the *last* thing I wanted was to become a part of it."

"I am an actor," he had told them, "not a politician. I am in show business."

But they would not take "no" for an answer. He finally agreed to spend the next six months on the road in California, making speeches. And if at the end of that time, based on audience reactions, it appeared he would be the best candidate, he would run.

The six months came and went. Reagan spoke from one end of the state to the other. The conclusion was inescapable: he must run. He did run.

His opponents tried to taint him as being merely an "actor in makeup." In an appearance on NBC's *Meet the Press*, Reagan got them back. He told the audience that ever since his first movie thirty years ago, the makeup people at Warner's had told him makeup wasn't good for him on screen, so he never wore it. Then he pointed out that everyone else in the studio that day, from his opponent Governor Brown to all the reporters on the panel, was wearing makeup.

They ridiculed him again as an actor who was merely delivering speeches written by someone else. It wasn't true; Reagan wrote his own speeches, but he realized it would be hard to prove. So he challenged Governor Brown to one-on-one "Town Hall" type debates that would obviously prove he could speak on his own. Brown refused the challenge.

Reagan won over voters in particular by his stance against Brown's liberal record and policies. People were disturbed by deadly riots that had broken out in the Watts section of Los Angeles, and the ongoing anti-Vietnam War disturbances at the University of California at Berkeley, which were sparked by liberal ideologies. Reagan's conservatism was a breath of fresh air. He won handily by more than a million votes.

As governor of California, Reagan tried to set into motion the ideas and ideals that he had been speaking about for years to the GE crowd and other groups. It turned out to be even more difficult than he had expected.

First, he discovered to his horror that the state of California was flat broke. The previous administration had cooked the books. Reagan slashed everything he could: he sold Governor Brown's private airplane, stopped out-of-state travel by government employees, canceled planned purchases of cars and trucks, and put a hold on new construction projects. Next Reagan called on the best businessmen in the state to try to unravel the mess and find a way to fix it.

In the end he was forced to do the one thing he abhorred: to ask for a tax increase. He did it, and he got it. It made him want to throw up. But two years later, between his cutting the bloated state budget and the tax increases, Reagan was informed that there would be a budget surplus of more than $100 million the next year. Budget director Caspar Weinberger wanted to know how to spend the money. Reagan didn't skip a beat. "Give it back to the people," he said.

Weinberger was astonished. "It's never been done," he said.

"You've never had an actor up here before, either," Reagan replied.

Reagan knew he couldn't refund the money directly to the taxpayers simply by writing them a check. That required approval of the legislature. "And if there was one thing I'd learned about government," he said, "it was that if there was any loose money lying around, the people in government would find a way to spend it." *Not* spending it was "the worst sin in a bureaucracy," because it meant the bureaucracy didn't need the money in the first place.

So what to do? No one in the legislature, Reagan learned, knew about the $100 million surplus. And he wasn't about to tell them. Instead, before the legislature could find out, Reagan went on radio and television and informed the taxpayers of the surplus. He told them that he could not refund the money without approval by the legislature, but since it amounted to about 10 percent of all revenues collected, the next time the people paid their taxes, they could simply subtract 10 percent of their tax bill, and so get their money back.

It was a delicious scheme, and as he'd predicted, the legislature went crazy. Reagan's novel proposal for returning the money was probably also illegal unless okayed by the legislature, but there was nothing they could do about it. They had been foiled! For when the people heard that they were going to get their money back, they were deliriously happy, and no legislator in his right mind would have refused to honor Reagan's plan.

Reagan was governor of California during the "wild 1960s," when a minority of students opposed to the Vietnam War and practically every vestige of adult authority were running rampant at colleges and universities across the country. California's colleges were among the hardest hit, with "strikes," rioting, building burning, bombing, and other violent acts. Reagan cracked down. He ordered the California National Guard to protect the campuses. He fired the president of the University of California system, because he refused to control the students. In retaliation, a group of radical students promised Reagan a "bloodbath." He suggested that they "start by taking a bath."

Campuses were festooned with banners that said, "Make Love, Not War." Reagan remarked that the students didn't look like they could do either one very well. He treated these students like spoiled children. Still, he was incensed that they were willing enough to enjoy the country's freedoms and opportunities, but weren't willing to defend them. They seemed to show an utter contempt for middle class and working class values, such as patriotism, respect for American values, and even football—all of which he took personally. In fact, as one of Reagan's biographers put it, "They didn't just despise the average American, they despised American ideals."

One day an organization of student leaders from the nine campuses of the University of California System asked to see Reagan. He was delighted, but when he entered the room he recalled that they appeared a motley crew, "Some were barefoot, and several were wearing worn T-shirts… some sprawled out on the floor. No one stood up."

Their spokesman began to upbraid Reagan, saying,

> Governor, we want to talk to you, but I think you should realize that it's impossible for you to understand us…. It's impossible for the members of your generation to understand your own children…. You weren't raised in a time of instant communications or satellites and computers solving problems in seconds that previously took hours or days or even weeks to solve. You didn't live in an age of space travel… of jet travel or high speed electronics…

Reagan looked at the student when he stopped for a moment to catch his breath and replied:

> *You're absolutely right. We didn't have those things when we were your age. We invented them.*

CHAPTER TEN

MISTER PRESIDENT

After Reagan's two terms as governor expired in 1974, he and Nancy bought a beautiful piece of ranchland, nearly 700 acres in the Santa Ynez Mountains north of Santa Barbara. It wasn't a long drive from their Los Angeles home, and they planned to use it on weekends or vacations so that Reagan could indulge his love of horseback riding.

But as soon as he left office, the phone began to ring almost off the hook. Prominent Republicans wanted him to run for president in the 1976 election. Reagan had mixed feelings. On the one hand, he was now in his mid-sixties and had accumulated enough money to live a comfortable retirement, and the job of president of the United States was one of the most demanding in the world.

On the other hand, even when he was governor, he was appalled at what he saw happening to his country. He had come to believe that the size and grasp of the government in Washington was now an even greater menace to the people's rights and liberty than it had been twenty years ago when he was making speeches for General Electric.

It seemed to Reagan that Washington "was trying to turn the states into nothing more than administrative districts of the federal government." Congress levied income taxes on the citizens and businesses, and then doled the money back out in various forms of "aid": aid to schools, aid to farmers, aid to businesses, to the poor, to highway projects, construction projects, and any number of other programs it saw fit to vote on. The average worker was now working for nearly four months out of the year simply to pay various kinds of taxes.

Worse, Reagan said, when the Washington bureaucrats took over the administration of these programs, "They began trying to dictate to Americans what they could and could not do." The regulations that came with these programs, he said, "were composed of so many rules that the states really weren't administering the programs, they were just following orders." Congress, he went on, might have passed a bill for a new program in good faith, but when they turned it over to the bureaucratic agencies to run, the bureaucrats "almost always responded by telling states, cities, counties, and schools *how* to spend this money."

The result, Reagan charged, was that state and local governments were "captives to a relentless Washington and a faceless federal bureaucracy that claimed to know better how to solve the problems of a city or a town than the people who lived there." In the old days for example, he said, "If parents didn't like the way their schools were being run, they could throw out the school board at the next election." But what could they do now about "the elite bureaucrats in the U.S. Department of Education who sent ultimatums into their children's classrooms regarding what could be taught, and what they could and could not read?"

Reagan had a big decision to make, and as he always said, for making big decisions there was nothing like being on the back of a horse. High in the mountains, at the big ranch they called "Tip Top," Reagan kept his favorite horse, Little Man, a large black thoroughbred. A splendid rider, Reagan liked to jump timber and dash across open fields, but on this particular day he simply ambled along. He reflected on the country's Founding Fathers, of what they would have made of the huge bureaucratic government now installed in Washington. They would have hated it, he concluded; their vision of the nation had been lost. Before the ride was over, he decided to run for president.

★ ★ ★

It was a very long shot. After all, the current president was a Republican himself, Gerald Ford. Reagan had covered him as a sportscaster when Ford was an all-star tackle for the University of Michigan. Reagan came close in that election, but lost his Republican party's nomination to Ford by a vote of 1,070 to 1,187. Ford, in turn, wound up losing the general election to the Democrat Jimmy Carter. It would be four more years before Reagan could run again. He did. And this time he won.

Under Jimmy Carter's administration, the U.S. economy had become a shambles. The price of gold skyrocketed, because people lost faith in the value of the paper dollar. Monetary inflation—the value of the dollar in relation to prices—had skyrocketed as well, so that where a year or so before a dollar would buy, say, a loaf of bread, or a half-gallon of milk, now it took two or even three dollars to purchase those things. Wages were not keeping up. People saw their savings becoming worthless. Interest rates (the percentage of money banks charge to borrow money for homes, cars, and every other thing), had soared from a reasonable 5 or 6 percent to over 20 percent. The housing market collapsed; businesses went broke. It was a near disaster.

In the midst of this there was an oil crisis with the Middle East nations, which in turn produced a gas crisis in the United States. People had to wait in long lines to fill their tanks, if gas could be had at all, and it was very expensive.

Worst of all, a mob of lunatic Islamic "militants" in Iran seized the U.S. embassy there and held the diplomats captive, threatening to kill them. For nearly a year and a half, Carter was unable to get them freed. It was widely viewed by Americans as an insult and a humiliation when such a powerful nation as the United States could not free American hostages being held by a puny, screwball, third world country.

Carter was helpless and hapless against these onslaughts. The public recognized the strength of Reagan's policies, and his successes as California's governor. Americans were ready for a strong leader. Reagan easily unseated Carter as president.

★ ★ ★

On Reagan's first day in office, the Iranians freed the American hostages, whom they had kept captive for nearly a year and a half. The incident has poisoned relations between the two countries ever since, but on January 21, 1981, the American people let out a collective sigh of relief.

President Jimmy Carter had told the people during his term in office that there was a "crisis of confidence" in America. True to form, Reagan told them instead: "Government is not the solution to the problem; government *is* the problem."

He knew the country he had been elected to lead was in bad shape, and it wouldn't be easy to put it right. What he didn't know was just how bad a shape the country was in.

Not only was the economy a shambles, but when he sat through a briefing about the U.S. military, he came away positively frightened. Nearly half the Navy's ships couldn't sail, and half the Air Force planes couldn't fly because of lack of spare parts, fuel, and crewmembers. He was appalled to learn that in the modern age of technological warfare, the vast majority of the enlisted men in the military were high school dropouts.

Meanwhile, the Soviet Union was modernizing and expanding their armed forces on an unprecedented scale. Its military was nearly twice as powerful as ours, both in numbers and weapons. Their forces were far larger than what would be needed to defend their own country, so the only reasonable conclusion was that their military buildup was designed for aggressive action elsewhere—possibly against the West.

But the most alarming revelation of all was the condition of our nuclear arsenal. Until the 1960s, the United States outnumbered the Soviet Union more than ten to one in nuclear missiles. By the 1980s, however, when Reagan took office, the Soviets outnumbered the U.S. in up-to-date computerized atomic weapons. Worse, our missiles were so old, and their technology so antiquated, that the theory of Mutually Assured Destruction, or MAD, no longer applied. Under the MAD hypothesis, each side could in theory destroy the other, so there would be no point in starting a war. Now, the military told Reagan, the Russians could actually win a nuclear war against the United States, annihilating more than half of the U.S. population in the process.

These were all difficult and expensive problems to fix. Reagan's first priority was the military and its nuclear arsenal. Next, to get the economy rolling again, he proposed a major cut in income taxes: 30 percent over the next three years.

His theory on why the tax cut would help the economy stemmed from his days as an economics major at Eureka College, and his experience with having to pay high taxes as a movie star. The American income tax system had originally been designed to be "progressive," meaning that those who made little or no income would pay the least, and those who made the most income would pay the most. The income tax had seemed reasonable in 1914 when it was first imposed—7 percent on incomes more than $500,000 ($10 million in today's dollars). But through various changes in the law over the years, the percentage—especially in the higher income brackets—had grown so large at one point that it was taking more than 90 cents on every dollar earned. "Any system that penalizes success and accomplishment is wrong," Reagan declared.

"Any system that discourages work, discourages productivity, discourages economic progress, is wrong."

"If... you reduce tax rates and allow people to spend or save more of what they earn, they'll be more industrious; they'll have more incentive to work hard, and money they earn will add fuel to the great economic machine that energizes our national progress. The result: more prosperity for all—and more revenue for government."

Some economists, and soon the media, labeled this notion or theory "supply-side" economics, which they eventually renamed "trickle-down" economics. Soon enough the media added another name of ridicule—"Reaganomics." They criticized the plan as being unworkable and a free ride for the wealthy. Reagan responded: "I just call it common sense," pointing out that President John F. Kennedy, a Democrat, had thought the same thing twenty years earlier when he pushed a tax cut through Congress.

Reagan found out soon enough that he would have formidable opposition to his programs in Congress, which was controlled by Democrats. "You're in the big leagues now," Tip O'Neill, the long time Democratic Speaker of the House of Representatives, informed him. It was not a friendly observation.

Within weeks of taking office, Reagan sent legislation drawn up by the White House staff that called for a 30 percent across-the-board income tax cut for citizens. Additional legislation called for a reduction in bureaucratic regulations on businesses and government programs, as well as large cuts to the fiscal budget that would offset any revenue lost by the tax cut.

Many Democrats were outraged. Tip O'Neill exclaimed to the press that Reagan's tax proposals would bankrupt the U.S. Treasury, and that his requested budget cuts would cause little old ladies to have nothing to eat but canned beans, or even to starve to death!

A few weeks earlier, Reagan had invited O'Neill to dinner at the White House, and they had an amiable evening swapping Irish jokes, telling stories, and getting acquainted in general. Afterward, Reagan said, "I thought I had gained a friend." In reality, he was in for a hard lesson of the "you're in the big leagues now" variety.

When Reagan learned what O'Neill was saying about him, he called the Speaker's office to ask what had happened to their good relationship. Tip told him: "Ol' buddy, that's politics. After six o'clock we can be friends, but before six, it's politics." Reagan said afterward that whenever he had dealings with O'Neill he was tempted to set his watch to six o'clock.

But Reagan had an ace in the hole. Because of Carter's miserable performance as president, a number of Republican senators had ridden into office with Reagan's election, and the Republicans now had a slim margin of control in the Senate. Republicans had gained in the House of Representatives, too, but not enough to take control.

However, Reagan himself—and the programs and policies he had successfully campaigned on—was so popular that several dozen Democratic congressmen banded together to work with him on his programs in the House of Representatives. They were mostly from the South, and took to calling themselves "Boll Weevil Democrats," after the worm that destroys the cotton plant from within. Fume as he might against these renegades, O'Neill and the rest of the Democratic leadership in the House could do nothing about them, nor change their minds. Combined with the Republicans, the Boll Weevils swung the balance for Reagan.

A brief word here about the legislative process in Washington. The president, or any member of the Senate or the House of Representatives, can introduce legislation. Once proposed, it goes before a committee in the House of Representatives to be discussed and modified as needed. Once the final bill is produced, the House votes on it. If it passes the House, the bill moves to the Senate where it is assigned to another committee. If that committee releases the bill, the Senate also votes on it.

If the bill passes the Senate vote, it goes to a joint conference committee of both the House and the Senate and, after further discussion and modification, the House and the Senate again vote on it. If the bill passes both houses in the second round of voting, it goes to the president, who has ten days to sign it into law or veto it. If the president vetoes the bill, it takes a two-thirds majority in each of the chambers of Congress to override the veto, after which the bill becomes law. If a two-thirds majority cannot be reached, the bill dies, and the process must begin anew, if at all.

During his time as president, Reagan would get much of what he wanted, but not necessarily when he wanted it. For example, it took until 1986, well into his second term, for Congress to pass his tax cut bill, and then with a 25 percent reduction instead of 30 percent.

Meanwhile, many Democrats, the liberal establishment in general, and the national media in particular, continued to rage against him with fury. Clark Clifford, a prominent lawyer and a fixture in Democratic administrations for several decades, famously referred to Reagan as "an amiable dunce." The newspaper columnist Jimmy Breslin accused him of "senility" and called him "shockingly dumb." A fellow Hollywood actor referred to his "low order of intelligence," while the newspaper *USA Today* announced: "It will take a hundred years to get the government back into place after Reagan."

This last might have been music to Reagan's ears; he would have hoped it would take five hundred—even a thousand years—before *that* kind of government would reappear. If these cruel gibes hurt him, he never showed it. "Amiable dunce" or not, he was at least "affable," which only seemed to further infuriate his enemies. A very self-important ABC News reporter named Sam Donaldson particularly enjoyed shouting rude questions at the president, but Reagan usually trumped him by laughing him off.

Having spent nearly thirty years as a Hollywood actor, Reagan knew about critics—movie critics or otherwise. He understood that ultimately what counts is the take at the box office: it was the public verdict that mattered. But reading over some of the mean-spirited things people said about him, it's hard to believe they didn't hurt his feelings, at least a little bit.

His first two months in office had been eventful and enlightening, but what happened next nearly cost him his life.

CHAPTER ELEVEN

A BLINK BETWEEN LIFE AND DEATH

On a bright spring day, March 30, 1981, Reagan had just finished speaking to a trade union convention and was about to enter the presidential limousine scarcely a mile from the White House. Suddenly shots rang out—six in all, in less than ten seconds. A Secret Service agent threw himself between Reagan and the shooter and got shot in the chest. At first Reagan thought the noise was firecrackers, but immediately two other burly agents plowed into him, literally knocking him into the back seat of the car and pinning him to the floor as they sped away.

For a moment Reagan felt the most severe pain of his life, and thought the agents had broken a rib or even his back. The limo driver was racing back to the White House when the Secret Servicemen let the president sit up. A stunned Reagan pulled a handkerchief from his pocket and let out a cough. "I must have cut the inside of my mouth," he said, but when the agents saw that the handkerchief was filled with red bubbly blood, they told the driver to head to George Washington University Hospital, on the double.

It was only a few blocks, but Reagan began to go pale and then gray; he couldn't seem to breathe properly and continued to cough up blood. At the emergency entrance he refused to be helped from the car; instead he stood, adjusted his pants, jacket, and tie, and began walking toward the doors like an actor coming onstage. He made it a few yards before collapsing into the arms of waiting staff, who rushed him inside to a gurney and into the ER.

His body signs began to sink, but no one could find any gunshot wound; it was thought he must have a broken rib that punctured a lung, and someone muttered it might be a heart attack. Reagan momentarily lost consciousness, but regained it. Doctors from all over the hospital rushed into the room in a panic. Outside, other wounded were being brought in to the emergency room. James Brady, the president's press secretary, was wheeled past Reagan. Somebody said he would probably die. Reagan said a prayer for him. Brady had been shot in the head. (He lived, but was paralyzed for the rest of his life.) They also brought in the Secret Service agent who was shot in the chest, and a D.C. police officer who had been shot in the throat.

Still nobody could find any wound on Reagan, but his lungs were quickly filling with blood, and he couldn't get enough air. So they X-rayed him again and there, under his right armpit, found a tiny little hole—more like a slice—bloodless, almost imperceptible, where the bullet had entered and sealed its own wound. It was a deadly, exploding bullet, which, had it actually exploded, most likely would have killed him almost instantly. They operated immediately, and just before he was put under anesthesia, Reagan murmured to the doctor: "I hope you're a Republican."

"Today, Mr. President, we're all Republicans," was the reply.

Few Americans knew at the time just how close their president had come to death. Somebody told him the would-be assassin had been captured, and that he was crazed. As Reagan lay on the hospital gurney, staring at the ceiling, he recorded later in his diary that he began to pray.

"But I realized I couldn't ask for God's help while at the same time I felt hatred for the mixed-up young man who had shot me.... I began to pray for his soul...."

They found the bullet with a probe and took it out, and repaired the damage to the lung, which had collapsed. It turned out the bullet was a ricochet that had bounced off the armor plate of the presidential limousine, flattened like a thin coin, and somehow flew through the open door of the car as Reagan was being shoved in it. It had lodged exactly one inch from his heart.

Nancy was at the White House when the head of her Secret Service team interrupted a meeting she was in and called her to the door. He said someone had tried to shoot the president, and that he was at the George Washington Hospital, but that they didn't think he'd been hit.

She rushed to the hospital, where a doctor told her he was in surgery. She tried to see him but was refused. So she found a chapel at the hospital and prayed. Then she tried to reach their children in California, and Michael and Maureen from his marriage to Jane Wyman.

When the surgery was over she was waiting, standing over him in the recovery room with doctors and nurses. He opened his eyes and said, "Honey, I forgot to duck." Everybody cracked up.

His recovery wasn't easy; the bullet had done a lot of damage. His lungs continued to leak, and he was pinned to the bed by tubes. He couldn't talk, and for days had to write notes to be understood. Some were funny. Nancy kept them, and years later showed them to one of his biographers, Peggy Noonan: "If I had this much attention in Hollywood," he had written in one of them, "I would have stayed there."

In the nation's history, four U.S. presidents have been assassinated, and seventeen others have had attempts made upon them, usually by crackpots or other deranged persons; the man who took the shots at Ronald Reagan and his party was no exception. Thirty-one-year-old John Hinckley had been swept up in weird delusions involving the movie actress Jodie Foster and wanted to make a name for himself to impress her. At his trial he was ruled insane, and today he is free on conditional release.

★ ★ ★

Reagan's recovery was painful, but within a few weeks he was back at work part time. Then, barely six months into his first term, Reagan was confronted with the first domestic crisis not left over from the previous administration. More than 17,000 air traffic controllers went on strike, bringing commercial air travel almost to a halt. As part of their contract, all government workers sign an agreement not to go on strike. The air traffic controllers' strike literally paralyzed the nation. Passengers were stranded all over the world, and few could get anywhere in the United States, except by using ground transportation.

Reagan told his diary on August 5, 1981, "That's against the [Taft-Hartley] law. I'm going to announce that those who strike have lost their jobs and will not be re-hired." Next morning he did exactly that, at a press conference in the White House Rose Garden, during which he gave the union members forty-eight hours to return to their posts or be fired. Couldn't get much plainer than that, and it sent everyone into a dither.

The union bosses were flabbergasted by the ultimatum; they hadn't seen anything like it in thirty years, since President Harry Truman had told striking railroad workers he was going to put them all in the Army and send them to the Korean War. Many of Reagan's own advisors were also upset, worrying that it might poison the administration's relationship with the labor movement. But Reagan held firm, and the country backed him. He'd been a union president himself, at the Screen Actors Guild, and he didn't countenance illegal strikes.

About 5,700 of the striking controllers grudgingly returned to work before the 48-hour deadline, but to the shock and disbelief of the ones who didn't, Reagan fired them, just as he had promised. "We've learned we've had about 6,000 more air controllers than we need," he confided to his diary on August 5. It let Americans know that, like it or not, their president was a man of his word.

★ ★ ★

On most weekends, Reagan would take Nancy and various aides and advisors and head up to Camp David, in the mountains of western Maryland, usually traveling in the presidential helicopter, "Marine One." It was a time to relax and watch old movies, cook out, and take long walks in the woods, but usually there was work to do, too, and Reagan would bring it with him.

It's not surprising that he looked forward to these getaways, considering what a president has to endure. Below is a list, based on his daily diaries, of a typical day in the life of a president of the United States:

February 23
1. Awakened in middle of night by huge explosions that "sounded like the War of 1812" (when the British Army burned the White House, Capitol, and other government buildings). Turned out to be a midnight fireworks celebration on the Mall (in front of the White House) in honor of Washington's Birthday.
2. Met with congressional leaders over proposed budget cuts and taxes.
3. Presented with silver medal by Capitol Historical Society, in honor of George Washington's Birthday.
4. Presented with Gold Helmet award by American Veterans, which had been postponed due to the assassination attempt.
5. Lunch with newspaper columnist George Will.

6. Meeting with the emissary of the Japanese prime minister about trade restrictions.
7. Meeting with cabinet regarding exports of grain.
8. Met with the Governor of Texas about the Energy Department.
9. Phoned presidents of Mexico and Venezuela regarding the Organization of American States (OAS).
10. Phone conversation with Canadian Prime Minister Pierre Trudeau on the situation in the Caribbean.
11. Attended a state dinner for U.S. governors.

If Camp David was a tonic for these long and tiring schedules, Reagan's California mountain ranch was a miracle restorative. He and Nancy would fly there on Christmas, Easter, Thanksgiving, and other long holidays. Many people assumed the ranch was a large elegant home with all the trappings, but in fact it was a simple one-story, three-bedroom adobe stucco affair with a red tiled roof, built by a Hispanic farmer in the 1890s. It was ten miles off the highway on a steep one-lane road that wound 2,000 feet above sea level, past citrus and avocado farms, and across a stream that had to be forded. The Reagans had modernized it and built a two-room guesthouse so visitors would have somewhere to stay, but all in all it was rustic, in a comfortable, homey sort of way.

The property was sizable, nearly 700 acres, with magnificent views of the mountains and the Pacific in the distance, and laced with well-kept riding trails, an olive orchard, and fields of wildflowers. Reagan kept horses here, and he and Nancy often went riding. Reagan rode in an English-style saddle, dressed in tall English boots and riding breeches, but most everyone else, including Nancy, rode Western, in a "cowboy" type saddle. Reagan liked to gallop and jump over timber, but when he became president, they made him stop jumping. Still, the mornings were reserved for trail rides; Nancy, the president, and whatever guests were there would saddle up with, of course, a squad of Secret Service agents tagging along.

Reagan liked to work on the ranch himself. He enjoyed building or repairing fences or cutting brush along the horse trails. He liked working with his hands and didn't mind getting dirty. For him, it was a kind of therapy after the cares of being president.

And of course, whether at the White House or the ranch, he enjoyed a good joke. As soon as he became president, the TV networks staked out positions on nearby hills, hoping their cameras would catch him riding or walking or doing something, anything, that would make the news. One of Reagan's speechwriters and biographers, Peggy Noonan, tells the story of the time Reagan became annoyed at the CBS network because it had begun filming him using an extremely powerful camera lens that could actually look through the windows of his house—and did! Reagan disliked this invasion of his privacy.

"So one day," according to Noonan, "knowing they were up there with the lens, the president went out the front door, walked onto the patio, grabbed his chest and fell to the ground pretending to have a heart attack. He lay there for a few seconds as far away producers shouted and cameramen tried to load their film. They were grabbing their phones to the networks when Reagan got up, waved to them in a jolly way and clicked his heels." He considered it one of his better performances.

★ ★ ★

By the autumn of 1983, big trouble was brewing for Reagan in the Middle East. The area had been a hotbed of danger and strife ever since the recognition of the State of Israel after World War II by the United Nations. Jews fleeing from persecution in Europe and Russia had been settling in Israel since early in the century. But it was still a predominantly Arab land.

The day after Israel became a state back in 1947, five surrounding Arab countries attacked it and were defeated. In the process, most of the Palestinians in Israel left. There are conflicting stories about why—some say the Palestinians were expelled by the Israelis, others that they left of their own accord. Most of the surrounding Arab states, however, refused to accept the Palestinians, and several hundred thousand wound up in the small, troubled country of Lebanon, which lies on the Mediterranean, bordering Israel.

Beirut, Lebanon's capital, had once been dubbed the "Paris of the Middle East," when it was a colony of France. It was an unusual Middle Eastern nation due to its demographic, half Christian and half Muslim, but the French had managed to keep peace between the two factions. Lebanon was once a lovely country of olive and citrus groves, of white sandy beaches and swaying palm trees. But after World War II, the French gave up control of the country, and a civil war broke out between the Christians and the Muslims.

Other nations intervened, including the United States, and an uneasy peace was kept from the 1950s until the 1970s, when other, larger groups of Palestinians arrived, among them militant Muslims who vowed to overthrow Israel.

Soon another civil war broke out between the Christians and Muslims, the balance of power having been upset by the arrival of Muslim Palestinians. Again Western nations intervened, but to complicate matters further, the Soviet Union began supplying arms to the Muslims.

Because of its support for Israel, the United States was targeted as an enemy by Muslim extremist groups, and in April of 1983 a terrorist bomb exploded at the U.S. embassy in Beirut, Lebanon, killing sixty-four people, including many Americans. That night Reagan wrote in his diary, "Lord forgive me for the hatred I feel for the humans who can do such a cruel, but cowardly deed."

The Reagan family: father, Jack, and mother, Nelle; brother, Neil ("Moon"), and Ronald ("Dutch") in white.

Ronald Reagan as a young boy in Dixon, Illinois.

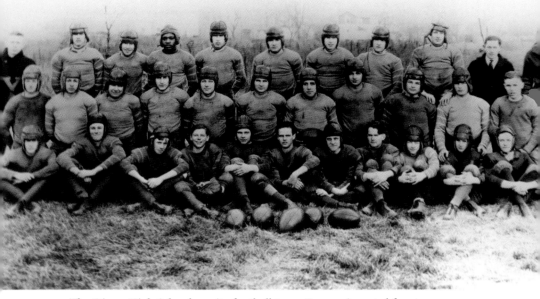

The Dixon High School varsity football team. Reagan is seated front row, fourth from the left. *Ronald Reagan Presidential Library*

Reagan as a lifeguard in his high school days. He was said to have saved more than seventy lives over several summers.

Ronald Reagan Presidential Library

Reagan was a standout football player at Eureka College in Illinois, where he also became passionate about politics and acting.

Reagan was captain of his college swim team (shown here on the right).

After college, Reagan became a well-known radio sportscaster in the Midwest. This eventually led him to Hollywood and fame.

Newly commissioned U.S. Army Cavalry Second Lieutenant Ronald Reagan and his proud mother, Nelle.

An excellent rider, Reagan loved to jump his horses. He had to quit, however, when he became president; the Secret Service said it was too dangerous. *Ronald Reagan Presidential Library*

Reagan in his performance in *Kings Row*. Shown here is the famous scene when he discovers he has lost his legs and cries, "Where's the rest of me?"

Reagan played the famous Notre Dame football player George "the Gipper" Gipp in the 1940 movie *Knute Rockne—All American*.

Just Married in 1952! Reagan and wife, Nancy, with the movie star William Holden as best man and Holden's wife at the time, actress Brenda Marshall (real name Ardis Ankerson).

Governor Ronald Reagan decorating a Christmas tree with Ron, Patti, and Nancy in their Pacific Palisades home, December 1967. *Ronald Reagan Presidential Library*

The Reagan family in the 1970s. From left, Patti, Nancy, Ronald, Michael, Maureen, and Ron.

Reagan and extended family at the White House at his first inauguration in 1981.

Reagan's first day as president: at work in the Oval Office.

Reagan's love of jellybeans was well known. Psychologists even tried to analyze his personality from the color of jellybeans he preferred. *Ronald Reagan Presidential Library*

In 1981 a deranged young man, who was trying to impress an actress, attempted to assassinate President Ronald Reagan. Reagan nearly died from his wound. Shown here is the chaotic scene after Reagan was driven away by the Secret Service.

With the Brandenburg Gate in the background, Reagan makes his famous "Tear down this wall" speech in Berlin, 1987. Two years later the wall came down, and Communism began to unravel in Europe and Russia.

Ronald Reagan Presidential Library

In 1988, Mikhail Gorbachev, the Communist premier of Russia, visited the United States. Reagan took him to see the Statue of Liberty.

Reagan on the White House lawn with then British Prime Minister Margaret Thatcher and his dog.

President Reagan throws the first pitch at a Chicago Cubs game. *Ronald Reagan Presidential Library*

Reagan, carving the turkey on Thanksgiving at the ranch with Nancy and his daughter Maureen.

President Reagan chopping wood at his ranch in the mountains near Santa Barbara.

Reagan at his favorite sport, riding, at the California ranch.

Reagan helping son Michael and grandchildren Cameron and Ashley build a snowman on the White House grounds, 1985.

Hard at work aboard Air Force One.

On his last day as president, Reagan stopped by the Oval Office for one last look. "Then," he said, "I was gone." *Ronald Reagan Presidential Library*

Reagan sent 1,800 U.S. Marines to the country to help quell the fighting, but in October, six months after the embassy bombing, a terrorist driving a large truck filled with explosives barreled through checkpoints and exploded into the Marine barracks at the Beirut airport. The blast killed 241 U.S. service members and injured many more. Reagan ordered the battleship USS *New Jersey* to the Mediterranean and had her fire her 16-inch guns at the hills around Beirut where the Muslim forces were concentrated. But four months later, he concluded that the situation in Lebanon was hopeless and brought the remaining Marines home.

No one is certain which terrorist group actually performed the bombing. A Muslim fundamentalist group from Iran claimed responsibility, but other intelligence sources think it was connected to the Palestinian terrorist group called Hezbollah. The Critics, of course, were waiting, and accused Reagan of being "stupid," "ignorant," and "foolish," in the way he handled the Lebanon affair. For his part, he said later that the Marine barracks bombing had "produced the lowest of the low points in my eight years in office."

CHAPTER TWELVE

STAR WARS AND THE EVIL EMPIRE

At about the time he learned of the Marine barracks bombing in Lebanon, Reagan was awakened at 4:00 a.m. by an urgent call from his national security advisor. A group of six island nations in the Caribbean Sea wanted immediate help from the United States to prevent a Communist takeover of the neighboring island of Grenada.

A week earlier, a group of radical Communists sponsored by Fidel Castro in Cuba had murdered Grenada's prime minister and were now conducting a large military buildup on the island, killing those opposed to them. The Organization of Eastern Caribbean States, composed of the nearby island states, was fearful that if Castro succeeded in Grenada, he would target them next.

For the past twenty-five years, the United States had endured a strained and unpleasant relationship with Castro, the revolutionary leader who overthrew Cuba's government in 1960, replacing it with a Communist regime with himself as its leader. He then allowed the Soviet Union to begin installing nuclear missiles in Cuba, aimed at the U.S. mainland.

The United States wasn't about to permit this, and President John F. Kennedy warned that any Russian ship approaching Cuba would be searched and turned back if any missile components were found. This led to the Cuban Missile Crisis, which brought America and the Soviet Union close to war. The crisis was defused when both sides backed down, and the Russians removed their missiles.

Meanwhile, Castro's government had taken over all U.S.-owned businesses in Cuba, so the U.S. issued an embargo on trading with Castro's Communist regime. The Cuban lifestyle went quickly downhill after that, even though the Soviets provided them with huge amounts of aid, financial and otherwise. The situation continued to simmer, and by 1980, the year before Reagan took office, Communists had overthrown the government in Nicaragua; Cuba was the Soviets' main outpost in the Western Hemisphere. U.S. intelligence agencies warned that the Soviets were relentlessly using Cuba as a jumping-off point to bring about Communist-style revolutions in other Central American countries—Guatemala, El Salvador, Honduras, Costa Rica, and possibly Mexico. Reagan was determined not to let that happen. So when the Organization of Eastern Caribbean States asked the U.S. for help, he decided they would give it.

There was one joker in the deck, however: 800 American students were then attending St. George's University School of Medicine in Grenada. Any action taken by the U.S. could wind up making them hostages of the Communists. Besides, if word leaked out of an impending U.S. operation against Grenada, it would give the nearby Cubans time to reinforce the Grenadan Communists.

Immediately, Reagan decided to conduct an operation to "rescue" the students and topple the Communist regime while he was about it. He demanded total secrecy—even the U.S. Congress would not be told, to keep the plan from leaking to the media.

"We didn't ask anybody, we just did it," he said afterward.

Two days later, nearly 2,000 Marines and Army Rangers landed successfully at two points on Grenada; only then did Reagan have the news announced to the media.

In the ensuing fight, nineteen American soldiers and Marines lost their lives, and another hundred were wounded. Castro had shipped hundreds of Cuban soldiers to Grenada, and at times the fighting was heavy. After the medical students had been rescued safely and the fighting died down, U.S. commanders took stock.

They found that the hundreds of Cuban workers who had been sent to Grenada allegedly to build a new airport for "tourism" had actually built a two-mile-long runway system designed to service Russian and Cuban military planes. They also found that the Cubans had shipped in enough arms and ammunition to supply thousands of "revolutionaries." And they found mountains of documents proving that the Soviets and Castro viewed Grenada simply as a stepping stone for the conquest of the Caribbean and Central America.

For their part, the people of Grenada greeted the American servicemen with flowers and banners that read, "God Bless America." Reagan felt proud. For the first time, he had "stopped the Communists in their tracks."

It would not be the last.

★ ★ ★

In a college commencement speech in 1982, Reagan told the students that the Soviet Union was in serious economic trouble because of the very nature of the Communist system of central control of everything. That might have worked well enough when most of its people were farmers. If they didn't produce, then they could starve (in the 1930s an estimated 30 million of them did).

Technology was king of the economic world by the second half of the twentieth century, but under a Communist system there would likely be no Bill Gates, Steve Jobs, or Michael Dell inventing and building computers in their garages. (For one thing, Soviet citizens had no garages, because they had no cars—but that's another story.)

Communism, Reagan told the students, had by its own design destroyed human initiative. There was no incentive for people to be industrious or efficient or innovative. They simply worked at what tasks they were given and accepted what the government gave them in return. And this in turn had made the Soviets unable to compete in the modern world. What was worse, Reagan said, the Soviet dictatorship had at the same time "forged the largest armed force in the world." And they had done it by spending upwards of half their entire economic output on their military, without regard for the needs of the people.

This, in a nutshell, was the situation Reagan faced when he took office. The Soviet Union was wounded, and he thought there might be some way to finish it off. But like wounded animals, Reagan knew the Soviets were highly dangerous, and he would have to be careful.

★ ★ ★

Unlike any president since the beginning of the Cold War thirty-five years earlier, Reagan actually believed there was some way, short of war, to destroy the Soviet Union. When the Soviets revealed their true intentions following World War II, American presidents had devised various policies to deal with them.

First was President Harry S. Truman's policy of "Containment," in which the United States would counter Communist aggression worldwide. This led to the wars in Korea and Vietnam. Next, in the 1970s, President Richard Nixon developed the policy of "Peaceful Coexistence," during which he opened trade with Communist China. The U.S. openly accepted the fact of large Communist powers in the world, and attempted to live with them, saying basically, "If you stay in your backyard, I'll stay in mine."

Next, toward the end of Nixon's administration, came the policy of *détente*, a French word literally meaning "to relax." This came about because both sides were concerned over the possibility of nuclear war, and they agreed to sit at a bargaining table and try to limit their arsenals. (Also, the Soviets hoped détente would offer them more trade with the West, particularly grain from the United States, since their system of collective farming was beginning to fail.)

Détente collapsed in the early 1980s during the Carter administration, when the Soviet Union invaded Afghanistan and the U.S. began giving aid to anti-Soviet forces there.

All of these policies accepted the existence of the Soviet Union into the eternal future, but when Reagan stepped into office, he brought a whole new perspective to the picture: he actually envisioned a world without Soviet Communism.

Getting rid of it would be a daunting task, to be sure, since the Soviets continued to maintain that the entire world needed to be brought under Communism. And not just *any* Communism, but a Communism controlled by the regime in Moscow. By the early 1980s, the Soviets had brought ten countries into their sphere in the past six years alone, either by outright invasion or by sponsoring revolutions. These countries were Angola, Ethiopia, and Mozambique in Africa; South Vietnam, Laos, and Cambodia in Southeast Asia; Yemen and Afghanistan in the Middle East; and Nicaragua and Grenada, which Reagan had just reclaimed, in the Western Hemisphere.

The first thing Reagan had to do was rebuild the U.S. military, for he knew the Soviets respected only strength. This would also be a difficult task. Democrats controlled the Congress and were very much against spending large sums of money for the armed forces. The Democrats were committed to social programs, and in the face of Reagan's tax cut proposals, they insisted there would not be funds enough for both an expanded military and their domestic agenda.

It was a long, tough fight, with many concessions and trade-offs that Reagan found distasteful, but in the end he and his political archenemy Tip O'Neill managed to work out funding for the military programs that Reagan insisted upon. These included a new state-of-the-art B-1 bomber, new naval ships, a new generation of up-to-date nuclear missiles called the MX "Peacekeeper," and substantially higher pay for the armed forces.

★ ★ ★

Reagan knew that at some point he was going to have to sit down with the Soviets to discuss matters. As a preliminary, he decided to let them know—and at the same time, to let the American people know—just how he felt. He began to make public statements on the Soviet Union and Communism which left no one in any doubt about his stance on the issue.

In the summer of 1982, he went to England and made a famous speech before the British Parliament in which he called the Soviet Union an "Evil Empire" that would soon be dispatched to "the ash heap of history."

Nine months later, in Orlando, Florida, he gave another speech in which he said: "If history teaches us anything, it is that simple-minded appeasement or wishful thinking about our adversaries is folly—it means a betrayal of our past, and the squandering of our freedom."

At Notre Dame University, he told the students: "The West will not *contain* Communism, it will transcend Communism. We will not bother to denounce it, we'll dismiss it as a sad, bizarre chapter in human history whose last pages are even now being written."

The Russians were stunned. The establishment media was indignant, and liberals far and wide branded Reagan a "warmonger," "insane," "foolish," "dangerous," and so forth. The *New York Times* accused him of trying to start a "Holy War."

Reagan's own State Department was horrified, fearing his comments would antagonize the Soviets and provoke them to do something rash.

The Department had earlier stricken those lines from his speeches, but Reagan personally reinstated them. He wanted to put the Soviet Union on notice that America was a force to be reckoned with. The United States was no pushover. Moreover, the United States "knew what the Soviets were up to."

He also wanted to define the Soviet Union in a way no other chief executive had defined it—in terms of right and wrong. Even though the notion initially caught flak from the political Left, in the end it resonated very well with the American people.

★ ★ ★

In 1967, back when Reagan was governor of California, he had paid a visit to the Lawrence Livermore National Laboratory that was operated by the University of California to develop nuclear weapons. There he met with the famous scientist Edward Teller, who was known as the "father of the hydrogen bomb." At the time, Teller was working on the development of space-based lasers which, he confided to Reagan, might some day be powerful and precise enough to demolish Soviet atomic missiles fired at the U.S. while they were still high above earth.

By the time he ran his campaign for president more than a decade later, Reagan assumed that some kind of laser defense against a Soviet nuclear attack would have been put in place. He was shocked, therefore, to learn otherwise when, in 1979, he visited the super-secret North American Aerospace Defense Command in Colorado. At the NORAD headquarters burrowed deep within a mountain, Reagan was briefed on the newest missile technology, which, he was told, could hit cities in Russia with almost uncanny accuracy.

But when Reagan asked what the U.S. could do if the Soviets fired a missile at an American city, the answer stunned him: nothing. Satellites and radar could track the thing from the time it was launched until the time it hit about fifteen minutes later, but other than that, the U.S.

military was helpless to stop it. Not only that, but such an attack would probably destroy the U.S. missiles before they could be fired from their silos, so, theoretically, the Soviets could actually "win" a nuclear war if they struck first, thus negating the whole premise of the MAD doctrine.

This nagged at Reagan all through his campaign. When he became president, he was informed early on in a top-secret meeting that, in the event of a nuclear war with the Soviet Union, the U.S. could expect to lose at least 150 million American lives—more than half the population—even if the U.S. "won." What was more, he realized, for any "survivors" of such a war, "the planet would be so poisoned, [they] would have no place to live."

Accordingly, one of the first things Reagan did following this revelation was to call a meeting of America's military leaders, the Joint Chiefs of Staff. He told them: "Every offensive weapon ever invented by man has resulted in the creation of a defense against it; isn't it possible in this age of technology that we could invent a defensive weapon that could intercept nuclear weapons and destroy them as they emerged from their silos?"

After a brief "huddle," the Joint Chiefs told Reagan that it was "an idea worth exploring."

Reagan's answer was, "Let's do it."

Thus the Strategic Defense Initiative (or SDI) was born. Later, when the strategy was revealed to the public, it would come to be known derisively in the press as "Star Wars," based on the popular movie trilogy.

★ ★ ★

In 1981 and 1982, Reagan met with Soviet leaders to talk about a reduction in nuclear weapons by both sides, but met with little success. The Soviets had installed within their borders a vast array of SS-20 medium-range nuclear missiles that could destroy all major European cities and most of Europe's population at the flip of a switch. Reagan said that unless those missiles were removed, he would, with the consent of the Europeans, deploy an equal number of U.S. Pershing medium-range missiles in Europe as counterbalance.

The Soviets became furious, and it was not until Reagan actually ordered the Pershing missiles shipped that the Soviets backed down and removed their missiles.

This issue caused a great uproar among certain pacifists and others both in Europe and the United States who demanded a nuclear "freeze," in which both sides agreed to produce no more nuclear weapons of any kind. While Reagan recognized that most of these people were well-meaning, he refused to enact a freeze. Owing to the overwhelming Soviet superiority in nuclear weapons at present, he said, a freeze would leave the U.S. completely vulnerable, and certainly in no position to bargain with the Russians over nuclear reductions.

But the advocates of a nuclear freeze were persistent. They picketed the White House by day and night, and held marches and rallies in cities all over Europe and America. Even Reagan's daughter Patti was among the protestors, which saddened him.

★ ★ ★

During his presidency, the media frequently made Reagan's relationship with his children a topic of discussion, and here is as good a place as any to examine it.

When Reagan entered the White House, his children from his first marriage, Maureen and Michael, were thirty-nine and thirty-six, respectively; from his second marriage, Patti was twenty-nine and Ron Jr. twenty-three. It had not been an easy time growing up, for anyone concerned.

After the divorce, Maureen and Michael had stayed with their mother, Jane Wyman, who sent them away to boarding schools because, as she told them, her busy acting schedule did not permit her to be a stay-at-home mother. Both children resented this, especially Michael, because he knew he was adopted, and the boarding school he attended was only ten miles from home. He developed emotional problems, flunked out of schools, wrecked cars, and was generally considered a loose cannon. After Reagan married Nancy, neither Maureen nor Michael got along with her very well.

Reagan tried to keep some semblance of a family relationship by taking all the children to his ranch for weekends, but more often than not there would be conflict lurking somewhere.

There were problems too with the children he had with Nancy (Patti and Ron) as they grew older. They also were sent to boarding schools, which also caused resentment. Patti in particular had difficulty adjusting to her father's new political career. When Nancy called her at school to say that Reagan had just been elected governor, she cried, "Oh no, how could you *do* this to me!"

That was in the 1960s, when many young people were rebelling against all established authority, and Patti was no exception. Her father represented all that she and her friends despised. At one point she told her half-brother Michael she was running away from boarding school because she had fallen in love with a restaurant dishwasher, and asked him to come and get her. Instead he called Reagan, for which Patti has apparently never forgiven him.

Later, her father's conservative politics so embarrassed Patti that she changed her name to Patti Davis, after her mother, and she posed nude for *Playboy* magazine. At the height of the nuclear freeze controversy, Patti asked her father to meet with the leader of the nuclear freeze movement, a Dr. Helen Caldicott. Reagan agreed, and they set up an hour-long meeting in the Oval Office. Afterwards Reagan wrote in his diary of Caldicott, "She is all steamed up and knows a lot of things that aren't true." For her part, after promising that she would say nothing publicly about the meeting, Caldicott promptly ran to the press with her version of the details.

The relationship between Reagan and his daughter remained strained until his death. After he left the White House, he wrote, rather plaintively, that he and Nancy had reached out to Patti, "But so far she's made it plain to me that she thinks I am wrong and that she is against everything I stand for.... I still dream and hope for a day when Patti and I will develop a close relationship again."

It was much the same with Ron Jr. He was expelled from boarding school, but managed to get into Yale for only one semester, after which he dropped out to become a ballet dancer. Subsequently he denounced his father's politics, proclaimed himself an atheist, dropped the "Jr." from his name, and joined the ultra-liberal radio show *Air America*.

One could probably spend a lifetime delving into the reasons for the Reagan family discord without arriving at an answer. Divorce was certainly a factor, especially since it was a bitter one. So was the divisive turmoil of the 1960s, at least in Patti's case.

None of this is to suggest that Reagan and his children were constantly at odds; there were flare-ups, but also many pleasant family holidays at the White House or the ranch. One just gets the feeling that everybody was walking on eggshells.

Reagan himself must share some of the blame. He was "old school," a stern taskmaster who certainly did not "spoil" his children. After Michael dropped out of college, Reagan told him that he was on his own to find a job and rent an apartment. When Maureen decided to run for the Senate, she was crushed to learn that her father would not endorse her in the Republican primary. He explained that it had always been his policy not to give endorsements for one Republican over another in Republican primaries, and he would make no exception—not even for his own daughter. (Maureen did not win her nomination contest, but she did rise to become co-chairman of the Republican National Committee while Reagan was still president, which pleased him greatly. Maureen died in 2001, of skin cancer.)

A thought that might be drawn from all this is that having a famous parent, or parents, is not necessarily a good thing, and most especially if divorce is involved. Families are sometimes fragile, and family life should be treasured, because there is *no substitute*. Parents, children—everyone—should take warning.

CHAPTER THIRTEEN

CHANGING THE RULES OF THE GAME

Reagan had a terrible time persuading Congress to fund the deployment to Europe of the MX missile, which would be more powerful and more accurate than anything the Russians then possessed. House Speaker Tip O'Neill and the Democrats didn't want to spend the money on the missile, arguing that it would be useless anyway because the Russians could destroy the U.S. missiles in their silos if they launched a first strike. Besides, the Democrats worried that building a series of mighty new missiles would be "provocative" to the Soviets.

Reagan thought so too. In fact, he *wanted* it to be provocative. The Soviets outnumbered the United States 2 to 1 or more in intercontinental ballistic missiles (ICBMs), and theirs had multiple warheads, so that a single Soviet missile could hit three or more American cities at once. Reagan believed that if he went to the bargaining table to ask for nuclear reductions, the Russians would laugh at him if he had nothing to bargain with.

In the end, Reagan got his missile, but barely. Congress voted 217 to 210 to fund the missile project, and Reagan got his bargaining chip. The new U.S. missile would also have multiple warheads—ten of them, each twenty times more powerful than the atomic bomb that was dropped on Japan in World War II—and a range of more than 5,000 miles. It became known as the "Peacekeeper."

Then, on March 23, 1983, Reagan stunned the world by revealing on national television that the U.S. was going to develop the Strategic Defense Initiative—"Star Wars." He told the people, "We seek neither military superiority nor political advantage. Our only purpose—one all people share—is to search for ways to reduce the danger of nuclear war."

The Russians, of course, were enraged, and denounced the idea as "insane," claiming that by developing a program to defend themselves against Russian missiles, Americans were somehow trying to "disarm" the Soviet Union.

In 1982 the Soviets walked out of arms reduction talks in Geneva, Switzerland.

"They'd left the ballpark," Reagan said, "but I didn't think the game was over. We had just changed the rules of the game. And they didn't like it."

But what the Russians did next defied reason and all bounds of human decency. On August 31, 1983, a South Korean commercial jumbo jetliner took off from New York bound for Seoul, the South Korean capital. It carried 269 individuals, including a U.S. congressman and sixty other Americans. Somehow, after refueling in Alaska, the plane wandered off course and into Soviet airspace.

Two Soviet warplanes picked it up and tracked it carefully in the bright moonlight. They were so close they would have been able to see the lights in the cabin, perhaps even the passengers themselves. Then, with no attempt to warn the jetliner, one of the Russian pilots told the other he had locked his air-to-air missile radar on the civilian plane and was going to fire. A few moments later, the Soviet pilot reported: "The target is destroyed." All 269 aboard were killed.

There was worldwide outrage at this unprecedented act of savagery, especially after the release of tape recordings of the conversation between the Soviet pilots.

The Soviets claimed that the jetliner was actually a U.S. spy plane, which was clearly ridiculous. How could anyone fail to recognize a Boeing 747 with civilian markings?

A furious Reagan told America that night: "It was an act of barbarism, born of a society which wantonly disregards individual rights and the value of human life, and seeks constantly to expand and dominate other nations.... If the massacre and [the Soviet Union's] subsequent conduct is intended to intimidate, they have failed in their purpose."

The incident served to further convince Reagan of the need to develop and implement Star Wars. He later wrote, "If... a madman got possession of a nuclear missile—we were defenseless against it. Once a nuclear missile was launched, no one could recall it."

★ ★ ★

During the four years Reagan had been in office, there had been three Soviet leaders—Brezhnev, Andropov, and Chernenko—and all three had died in office. They were, Reagan said, "Tough, old-line Communist[s] addicted to Lenin's secular religion of expansionism and world domination."

Negotiations were tough enough, but things were even more complicated by the fact that Reagan had no time to get to know the Soviet leaders. "How am I supposed to get anyplace with the Russians," he asked Nancy, "if they keep dying on me?"

The new man in the Kremlin in 1985 turned out to be a different kind of character. His name was Mikhail Gorbachev, and while he was a dedicated Communist, he was also a sensible man who saw clearly the dangers in having two powerful nations with a world-ending array of nuclear weapons pointed at each other. Reagan invited him to come to

Washington for nuclear arms reduction talks, but Gorbachev refused. Instead, as Reagan had predicted, he suggested that the two of them reconvene the Geneva Conference. The Soviets were back in the ballgame.

Reagan met Gorbachev on a cold November morning on the front porch of a lovely villa on Lake Geneva. Let him describe the encounter:

> As we shook hands for the first time I had to admit... that there was something likable about Gorbachev. There was warmth in his face and his style, not the coldness bordering on hatred I'd seen in most senior Soviet officials I'd met until then.

Reagan knew going in to the negotiations that it would be rough. "In strategic weapons," he wrote in his diary, "when the Soviets refer to 'maintaining stability,' they mean 'superiority,' and they have it." Reagan, however, had at least one ace in the hole, and that was his experience as a bargainer. All those years he'd been president of the Screen Actors Guild, he had had to sit across the table from the heads of the movie studios—Harry Cohn, Louis B. Mayer, Jack Warner, and the like. They were among the toughest negotiators in the world, and Reagan had learned much from the experience.

Previous U.S. presidents, in negotiating with the Russians, had spoken of arms *limitations*; Reagan wanted to talk about *reductions*, meaning that both sides would actually get *rid* of atomic weapons—destroy them—instead of just limiting the number each side could produce. That is what he had come to Geneva to discuss, but he didn't get far.

Before the Russians would even agree to talk about reducing nuclear weapons, they demanded that the U.S. remove the Pershing missiles it had deployed in Europe and abandon Star Wars.

Reagan proposed what he called a "zero-zero" option in Europe. The Soviets would remove their intermediate range missiles aimed at European capitals, and the U.S. would remove the Pershings. Gorbachev said no.

Regarding Star Wars, Reagan dropped another real stunner. If it turned out to work, Reagan said, he would open the U.S. laboratories to other nations, *including the Soviet Union*, and let them copy its Star Wars plan and implement it themselves! That way, Reagan told Gorbachev, the world would be free of nuclear weapons, for the simple reason that they wouldn't work. They would all be intercepted and destroyed high up in space.

Gorbachev replied that if the U.S. developed Star Wars, it could then launch a nuclear attack on the Soviet Union without fear of retaliation. In other words, he thought Reagan was lying.

While the dialogue accomplished little, Reagan nevertheless felt he could work with Gorbachev in the future. "I finally found a Soviet leader I could talk to," Reagan said. "He could tell jokes about himself and even about his country, and I grew to like him."

In the end, the two issued a joint statement saying that they were aiming at a 50 percent reduction in nuclear weapons, and that there would be more discussions.

For Reagan it was a big victory that he could announce to a joint session of Congress. "We are headed in the right direction," he told the legislators upon his return, to "enthusiastic cheering and stomping in the chamber of the House of Representatives."

Afterward, he wrote in his diary, "I haven't gotten such a reception since I was shot."

★ ★ ★

As it turned out, it wasn't that easy. The devil was in the details.

Reagan and Gorbachev had agreed to meet in Reykjavik, the capital of Iceland, to work out the fine points of a nuclear arms reduction agreement. The Soviet leader agreed to remove his country's medium-range missiles aimed at European cities and to reduce Soviet intercontinental missiles by 50 percent, beginning immediately, with the aim of destroying *all* nuclear missiles within ten years. This was music to

Reagan's ears. It was much more than he had expected, and his spirits soared until just before the end of the conference when Gorbachev added a condition: "This all depends, of course," the Soviet premier said, "on you giving up SDI [Star Wars]."

Reagan was shocked and outraged. He had already told Gorbachev that Star Wars wasn't on the table as a bargaining chip. "There's no way we're going to give up research to find a defense against nuclear weapons," he angrily told Gorbachev. And he reiterated what he had already told the Soviet leader—that if Star Wars was found to work, he would share it with the Russians and any other nation that wanted to defend itself against nuclear attack.

Gorbachev again told Reagan, in so many words, that he didn't believe him.

Reagan said, "The meeting is over." He turned to his secretary of state, George Shultz: "Let's go, George, we're leaving."

Reagan was furious. He realized that Gorbachev had gotten him to come to Iceland for one purpose only—to kill Star Wars. But he was encouraged, too, and wrote that night in his diary: "Well the ball is in his court and I'm convinced he'll come around when he sees how the world is reacting." What Reagan also realized was that the Russians were scared of Star Wars. Very scared—because it could cancel out all of their great advantage over the U.S. in nuclear weapons.

But he was wrong about the world's reaction, at least at first. The liberal media in the U.S. attacked him at once, running such headlines as "Sunk by Star Wars" and "Reagan-Gorbachev Summit Talks Collapse as Deadlock on SDI Wipes Out Other Gains." They said that he had botched an opportunity to secure nuclear weapons reduction agreements on an extraordinary scale, just for the sake of insisting on a questionable nuclear defense system.

He didn't care what the press said, or about his polling numbers, or about the sniping bureaucrats in his own administration. The night after he got home, Reagan went on national television with a speech he had written himself on the plane trip home. "There was no way I could tell our people their government would not protect them against nuclear destruction," he said, explaining why he thought Star Wars was necessary. It worked. Though the press continued its attacks, the people had listened, and polls showed they favored Reagan's position overwhelmingly.

★ ★ ★

That June, Reagan went to Berlin. He found the German capital strange and depressing, one half thriving and free, the other half held captive behind a totalitarian wall. He wondered what kind of government, "penned in its people like farm animals?"

He made a speech. It may be the most famous speech he ever gave. One would have to look back to Franklin Roosevelt's reaction to Pearl Harbor or John F. Kennedy's Berlin speech, or even Lincoln's Gettysburg Address to find anything comparable by an American president. He gave it in front of the Brandenburg Gate, which cut through the Berlin Wall near the center of the city. It's worth repeating parts of it here:

> Behind me stands a wall that encircles the free sectors of this city, part of a vast system of barriers that divides the entire continent of Europe. From the Baltic, south, those barriers cut across Germany in a gash of barbed wire, concrete, dog runs, and guard towers. Farther south there may be no visible, no obvious wall. But there remain armed guards and checkpoints all the same—still a restriction on the right to travel, still an instrument to impose upon ordinary men and women the will of a totalitarian state. Yet it is here in Berlin where the wall emerges most clearly; here, cutting across your city, where the news photo and the television screen have imprinted this brutal division of a continent upon the mind

> of the world. Standing before the Brandenburg Gate, every man is a German, separated from his fellow men. Every man is a Berliner, forced to look upon a scar....
>
> As long as the gate is closed, as long as this scar of a wall is permitted to stand, it is not the German question alone that remains open, but the question of freedom for all mankind. Yet I do not come here to lament. For I find in Berlin a message of hope, even in the shadow of this wall, a message of triumph....
>
> In the 1950s, Khrushchev [then the Soviet premier] predicted: "We will bury you." But in the West today, we see a free world that has achieved a level of prosperity and well-being unprecedented in all human history. In the Communist world, we see failure, technological backwardness, declining standards of health, even want of the most basic kind—too little food. Even today, the Soviet Union cannot feed itself.... there stands before the entire world one great and inescapable conclusion: Freedom leads to prosperity. Freedom replaces the ancient hatreds among the nations with comity and peace. Freedom is the victor.

Reagan told the crowd that in recent months the Soviets had given appearances of softening up somewhat, and wondered if it was the "beginning of profound changes in the Soviet state," or merely "token gestures, intended to raise false hopes."

And then he dropped the bomb, so to speak, with real anger rising in him now that he was seeing the wall in person.

> There is one sign the Soviets can make that would be unmistakable, that would advance dramatically the cause of freedom and peace.

General Secretary Gorbachev, if you seek peace, if you seek prosperity for the Soviet Union and Eastern Europe, if you seek liberalization: Come here to this gate! Mr. Gorbachev, open this gate! Mr. Gorbachev, TEAR DOWN THIS WALL!

The crowd at first was stunned. No one had ever talked like that—especially not a president of the United States. Berlin was completely surrounded by the Soviet-backed Communist government of East Germany, with all the dangerous armed force that fact implied. But the Germans suddenly and spontaneously burst into applause, and then cheers, and more cheers, and for some even tears. It was what they thought, what they wanted. He had said it for all of them. And he *was*, by damn, the president of the United States of America.

The State Department had tried to cut the "Mr. Gorbachev, tear down this wall" part of the speech. Like the "Evil Empire" line Reagan had used earlier, the State Department was afraid it would "provoke" the Russians and cause diplomatic trouble. Reagan just said: "I think we'll leave it in."

The U.S. media generally criticized the speech as "provocative," "unfortunate," "risky," and the Soviets predictably characterized it as "warmongering."

It would be two more years before the incensed and frustrated population of East Germany and other Soviet captive states took matters into their own hands and tore down the wall themselves, piece by piece. The delicious irony was that Reagan lived to see it.

CHAPTER FOURTEEN

"THEN I WAS GONE"

Ever since he arrived in the White House, the media had made a point of remarking that Reagan had no close friends. By that, they meant that he didn't chum around with anybody, not even people in his own presidential cabinet. They said it was an indication that Reagan was peculiar or out of touch. One of the charms of Reagan was that he didn't much care what was written or said about him on TV, which further infuriated the media.

The fact was, Reagan once had many close friends. They were movie stars such as William Holden, Robert Taylor, Dick Powell, Spencer Tracy, Robert Montgomery, Walter Pidgeon, Clark Gable, Gary Cooper, and others who in their time were among the most famous people in the world. But all had died, and most of them died young. If he'd had better sense, he might have made friends with younger people, but when you were old like Reagan was—in his seventies—it was hard to make new friends—at least close friends. His best friend now was Nancy. He trusted her, and she protected him from those she thought were trying to use him. The press simply didn't understand.

They wrote that he fell asleep in important meetings, despite the fact that cabinet members said this never happened. They made fun of him because he liked to eat jellybeans at cabinet meetings. They even got psychologists to analyze his method of eating the jellybeans—did he only select certain colors of jellybeans, or did he eat all colors? It was maddening, but only for the press, because no matter what they wrote, it seemed, he ignored them, and sometimes even made fun of them.

But there came a time when he could ignore the press no longer, because there were things afoot in his administration that Reagan did not know about. It was one of the most troubling episodes of his presidency and threatened to bring it down.

★ ★ ★

From the day he entered the White House, Reagan had been increasingly troubled by Communist intrusions in the Western Hemisphere, which were secretly sponsored by the Soviet Union. First, as discussed in chapter 12, there was the Communist takeover of Cuba, which in the 1960s had produced the Cuban Missile Crisis that brought the world to the brink of nuclear war. The Russians were constantly meddling in the Caribbean region. There was Grenada, as we have seen, but they also had attempted to stir up Communist revolutions in Guatemala and Panama, and most recently in Nicaragua, where during the Carter administration a Communist-backed group calling themselves "Sandinistas" (after a revolutionary hero) overthrew the country's tin-pot dictator and threatened to spread Communism throughout the region.

Opposing them was a group known as the "Contras," who were fighting to bring democracy to Nicaragua. Reagan helped them by sending U.S. aid, but in 1985 that effort was cut off by Democrats in Congress, who passed legislation making it illegal for the United States to provide assistance to the Contras.

What came next was a highly complicated series of events that wound up with Reagan being accused by the press and congressional Democrats of violating the prohibition against giving the Contras military assistance.

It began half a world away, when Islamic terrorists began kidnapping Americans in the Middle East and threatening to kill them unless the U.S. forced Israel to release Palestinian prisoners they were holding. It was almost as maddening for Reagan as it was for the kidnapped hostages' families. For all its might and power, the U.S. found itself unable to deal with a handful of scruffy terrorists. It almost seemed to fulfill Richard Nixon's 1970 mock description of the United States as "a pitiful, helpless giant."

In 1985, the Israeli intelligence service informed U.S. authorities that a group of "moderate" Iranians had told them they could get seven of the American hostages released if Israel would sell Iran a small number of anti-tank and anti-aircraft missiles that the United States had provided to Israel. Reagan agreed secretly to the deal, and the weapons were provided to the Iranians, even though it was official U.S. policy not to trade arms for hostages. In Reagan's mind, he wasn't going against policy, since the arms were Israeli-owned.

However, the Israelis had made the United States agree to sell them similar arms to make up for the loss, which it did. The Iranians released a single hostage, a Catholic priest—five others remained captive. Another either died or was killed by the terrorists. But still Reagan did not give up.

Next, Marine Colonel Oliver North, a military aide to Reagan's national security staff, proposed what he thought was a brilliant plan—have the U.S. sell the weapons directly to Iran at an inflated price, and use the pocketed profits to aid the Contras in Nicaragua. It might be illegal, but North thought they could get away with it on grounds that the law Congress passed (called the Boland Amendment) only specified that it would be illegal for the government to "appropriate" money for the Contras' use. North argued that no money would be appropriated, because he intended to "mark up" profits for the arms—to the tune of $20 million. The National Security Council approved North's plan without consulting Reagan, thinking it would neatly skirt the law.

It didn't. In 1986, a newspaper in Lebanon got wind of the deal and it became a full-blown, worldwide scandal. Congressional hearings were hastily called, and the media had a field day. Everyone wondered whether Reagan had violated the law. The editor of the *Washington Post* declared he "hadn't had so much fun since the Watergate scandal."

Reagan's national security advisor resigned immediately, and Reagan fired Colonel North. More than a dozen officials in the administration were indicted for such crimes as conspiracy, lying to Congress or to prosecutors, and destroying evidence. Eight were convicted, but none went to jail. They were either pardoned by the next president (George H. W. Bush), or their convictions were set aside for other reasons.

In the immediate aftermath of the scandal, Reagan saw his popularity drop twenty-one points in the polls—from 67 to 46 percent. As was his practice, he carried his case to the American people with a nationally televised speech in which he apologized and took "full responsibility" for the matter. He informed his audience that he had been attempting to free the hostages and make some sort of political inroad with Iran. Most importantly, he said that he did not know that any money was being funneled to the Contras in Nicaragua.

In 1987, a special commission cleared Reagan of any direct illegal activity in connection with the case, which came to be known as the Iran-Contra Affair. In the end, a total of three American hostages were released, but different terrorists soon captured others to take their places.

Aided by the money from the scandal, the Contras kept up their fight and in 1990 forced the Communists to hold elections. The Contras won, took control of Nicaragua, and installed a democracy. Reagan's popularity in the polls soon returned to normal, but the scandal remains a stain on his presidency.

★ ★ ★

In the midst of the Iran-Contra scandal, other problems, big and small, bedeviled the president as usual. One was the continued belligerence of the Libyan strongman, Colonel Muammar Gaddafi, an Islamic extremist who had disturbed the peace of the Middle East and elsewhere for nearly twenty years. He had seized control of Libya in a coup in 1969. At once he had imposed Islamic law there, expelled the Jews, declared Libya to be an "Islamic Socialist state," and began a systematic program of worldwide political assassinations.

Gaddafi's relations with the West were anything but cordial. He was believed to have been behind the terrorist massacre of eleven Israeli athletes at the 1972 Olympic Games in Munich. He was able to obtain supersonic MiG fighters and other modern weapons from the Soviets, and began a campaign of subversion and terror against his neighbors and abroad. Naturally, he denounced Israel, damned the United States in a *Time* interview, and declared on the Arab Al Jazeera TV network that, because of Muslim immigration, "Allah will grant Islam victory in Europe within a couple of decades."

In 1986, contrary to international laws of the sea, Gaddafi declared that the Gulf of Sidra in the Mediterranean was off-limits to the U.S. and other navies, and began firing missiles at American warships that entered the area. Meanwhile, Libyan "hit squads" had persisted in assassinations and bombings across Europe, including an explosion that wrecked a Berlin nightclub that was popular with American servicemen, killing three people and wounding two hundred, including fifty Americans. U.S. intelligence intercepted communications linking Gaddafi to the crime.

Reagan had had enough. Calling Gaddafi a "crackpot," he asked his Security Council and the Joint Chiefs of Staff how the U.S. could let the Libyan know that the U.S. wouldn't let him get away with this stuff—but "without harming innocent people." They settled on a plan to bomb Gaddafi's military headquarters and barracks in Tripoli.

The authorities in Great Britain agreed to support the operation. The U.S. jets would fly from bases in England, but France refused to let them cross French airspace, thus forcing the planes to make a 1,000-mile detour. "While [The French] publicly condemn terrorism," Reagan wrote, "France conducted a lot of business with Libya, and was typically trying to play both sides."

The U.S. attack was a success. Afterward, little was heard from Gaddafi for the next two years, but in December of 1988, terrorists put a bomb aboard a Pan Am 747 flying from the United Kingdom to the U.S. It exploded above Scotland, killing all 259 persons aboard and 11 on the ground in the village of Lockerbie. Evidence revealed Libyan involvement, and ultimately a lone Libyan man was tried and convicted of the crime. Gaddafi later renounced terrorism, but in 2010 he was suspected of being behind the release of the Pan Am bombing culprit from a Scottish prison. In 2011 the Libyans rose up and overthrew his regime, and Gaddafi was shot dead.

★ ★ ★

All the while, Reagan had been working behind the scenes to nudge Gorbachev toward a nuclear agreement. For three years, the two exchanged a series of extraordinary letters—extraordinary because Reagan not only revealed to the Russian leader the United States' understanding of Soviet nuclear capabilities, but American capabilities as well. Under normal circumstances these would be closely guarded state secrets, but Reagan—and presumably Gorbachev—both realized that U.S. and Soviet intelligence agencies already knew the information about one another.

But the letters are remarkable if only because no U.S. president had ever communicated with a Soviet leader on such an open and candid basis.

Meantime, it had become apparent both to Reagan and Gorbachev that the economy of the Soviet Union was in deep trouble. Because the Soviets had been throwing so much money into their vast military programs, they were now unable to feed their own people. Also, there was trouble brewing for the Communists in their satellite "puppet" states; anti-Soviet demonstrations had occurred in Poland, Hungary, Czechoslovakia, and elsewhere.

Gorbachev, however, alone among the Soviet leaders, had begun to liberalize the vast Soviet government. In 1987 he introduced a policy of *perestroika*, or "restructuring" of the Russian economy, that allowed a certain amount of free enterprise and permitted the capitalist concept of supply-and-demand to operate, overruling the once-sacred Communist doctrine of total central planning that had proved so disastrous to the economy.

Likewise, he decreed that the principle of *glasnost*, or "openness," would henceforth prevail in the Soviet Union, which would let the Soviet citizens see just what the government was doing. Prior to *glasnost*, there had been widespread corruption among the so-called "political classes" (members of the Communist Party), and *glasnost* was designed to expose it.

Gorbachev was one of the few Soviet leaders who was actually educated, having studied law and economics at Moscow University. This gave him critical insights where previous Soviet rulers—as well as many of his own contemporaries—clung to stale and failing communist dogma.

Old-line Communists were horrified at these new procedures, fearing they would bring down the state, and Communism itself. They did not believe the people were capable of appreciating either truth or freedom, but instead that they must be kept under the iron fist of the all-controlling Communist Party. Nevertheless, Gorbachev prevailed, and

Reagan was prompt to congratulate him on every loosening of the stern dictates of the Soviet system.

Privately, Reagan wrote that Gorbachev's *perestroika* was actually "a bill of particulars condemning the workings of Communism, as damning as anything ever written about Communism." In fact, as Reagan declared, "It was an epitaph: Capitalism had triumphed over Communism."

★ ★ ★

All throughout the exchange of letters between the two men, Gorbachev had steadfastly insisted that no nuclear agreement could be reached until the U.S. abandoned its notion of building the Star Wars protective space shield.

Reagan, however, stuck to his guns. In December of 1987, Gorbachev and his wife arrived in Washington, DC, to begin a new round of talks about reducing nuclear weapons. The Soviet leader had suddenly dropped his insistence that there could be no agreement unless the U.S. abandoned Star Wars. Reagan's reaction is contained in three words in his diary: *The Soviets blinked*.

When the new treaty was announced, Reagan's stock rose higher with the American public than ever before. It was the first time that two nations had agreed not only to remove, but actually to *destroy* nuclear weapons.

It wasn't only the United States that considered Reagan a hero. The Russian people did as well.

After the conference in Washington, Gorbachev invited Reagan and Nancy to visit Moscow, which they did a few months later. Everywhere he went in Russia, Reagan was mobbed by grateful Russians who, he said, "couldn't have been more affectionate."

"They were simply ordinary people," he wrote, "who longed for the same things that Americans did: peace, love, security, a better life for themselves and their children. On the streets of Moscow, looking into thousands of faces, I was reminded that it's not people who make war, but governments."

That night after the magnificent Bolshoi Ballet, Reagan wrote: "I knew the world was changing when we stood with the Gorbachevs in our box, with the Soviet flag on one side, and ours on the other, and 'The Star Spangled Banner' was played by a Soviet orchestra."

On the last day of his visit, Reagan was given the opportunity to address a packed audience of the brightest students at Moscow University. Another man might have felt restrained in the presence of his Communist host, but Reagan pulled no punches.

"Your generation," he told the students, "is living in one of the most exciting, hopeful times in Soviet history. It is a time when the first breath of freedom stirs the air... when the spiritual energies of a long silence yearn to break free."

He told them of the freedoms enjoyed by U.S. citizens, and of the wonders of capitalism—using as an example the founding of Dell computers, "by two college students no older than yourselves, in the garage behind their home." He added, "No single authority or government has a monopoly on the truth." He told them they had "the right to dream." They gave him a standing ovation.

★ ★ ★

Not long afterward, Reagan's second and final term in the White House ended. As the time drew near, he sometimes reflected on what he considered his failures.

Foremost among them was his inability to stem the growth of big government, let alone reverse it; his conclusion was that the political system had simply grown too powerful. It was his tax reform, and the decision to meet the Soviets head-on militarily, that trapped him. He had to make too many trade-offs with Tip O'Neill and the congressional Democrats, who knew trade-offs all too well.

Not only that, but the national debt piled up during his administration. He had pleaded with Congress for a line-item veto, meaning that a president—any president—could veto specific spending items in a national budget without having to veto the entire bill, which of course would shut down the country. His plea fell on deaf ears, however, and became another of his failures, and the budget deficit—as well as the national debt (what all Americans actually owe)—exploded during his term in office. He counted this as his "greatest disappointment."

Reagan also lamented his failure to forge some kind of settlement in the Middle East, which was just "as much a snake pit of problems as it was when I unpacked my bags in Washington in 1981."

Racial and religious hatreds in that ancient region have extra-long memories, as the world has subsequently seen. Reagan summed it up this way: "For eight years, I gave high priority to bringing lasting peace to the Middle East, but in the end it eluded me, as it had eluded other American presidents before me."

After Reagan and Gorbachev concluded the nuclear armaments treaty, Reagan genuinely feared for Gorbachev's life. When the Soviet leader visited New York a few months later, his Russian security staff was extremely worried that someone would try to assassinate him. Reagan assured them that the U.S. Secret Service would be protecting Gorbachev, too, but the Russians explained that they feared some Soviet assassin would make the attempt. On Gorbachev's final day in Manhattan, Reagan took him to see the Statue of Liberty.

There is not much for a lame-duck president to do during the final days in office. Once his vice president, George H. W. Bush, had received the Republican nomination, Reagan spent time on the campaign trail stumping for him. There were small parties for staff and friends. There was packing to do. George H. W. Bush won the election, and before the inaugural the Reagans held a reception for White House staffers.

Reagan had wanted to make a nice speech, "But when the band started playing 'Auld Lang Syne', we couldn't say much of anything," he said.

Next morning, before the inaugural ceremony, he found himself alone in the Oval Office. As he started to walk out, he turned halfway through the door for one last look.

"Then," he said, "I was gone."

CHAPTER FIFTEEN

THE LAST STAND ON EARTH

When Ronald Reagan entered the White House in 1981 as the fortieth president of the United States, he inherited a disastrous economy and turned it into a success. He did it mostly by lowering income taxes. In general, when taxes are low, the economy prospers, and the government earns more revenue.

It was Reagan's belief that when taxes are high, both businesses and personal income earners cut back. Jobs are lost, and businesses either fail or don't get started in the first place. Under Reagan's economy, the re-employment of workers followed, as did the end to inflation of the dollar, which had continued to make all things increasingly more expensive.

By the end of his presidency, interest rates—which had soared by the time he took office—were back to normal. So was unemployment. Government revenues from taxes were up, because the economy had begun to boom.

His most significant failure, by his own admission, was the inability to reduce the size, scope, and power of the government. As long as government kept on growing, taxing, and spending, he believed, America would never fulfill its promise as a truly free enterprise system.

Reagan got his tax policies through Congress because of his persuasive personality, his willingness to bargain, and his charismatic actor's ability to carry his points across the land through the medium of television, in which he was already well versed.

Unlike Theodore Roosevelt, Reagan did not "speak softly" in his foreign policy, but he did "carry a big stick." He used the power of his office as a "Bully Pulpit" to warn America and the world of the evils in Communism. And he backed up his talk with action.

He became commander in chief of a U.S. military that was moribund: undermanned, under-funded, under-motivated, out-classed, and outmoded. He had also inherited an extremely dangerous deficiency in nuclear arms capability. Meanwhile, the Soviet Union had spent countless billions upgrading and up-sizing its military forces, and had gone so far ahead in atomic weapons that if the Russians had decided to hit the U.S. with a "first strike," they would have destroyed the country.

Using his powers of persuasion, Reagan wheeled-and-dealed with Democrats in Congress to fund an upgrading of the American fighting forces. Here's what he told them, and bluntly: "If we lose freedom here, there will be no place to escape to. This is the last stand on earth."

Just as important, he convinced Congress to allow the military to build the MX "Peacekeeper" ballistic missile, which put the Russians on notice that they, too, would be destroyed in any nuclear attack on the United States.

But Reagan's trump card—his "big stick," which contributed heavily to the Soviet Union's collapse—was his announcement of Star Wars, the space-based protective shield program. Reagan knew it would be years in coming, if at all, but he used it as a lever with Mikhail Gorbachev, who finally realized that the Soviets could never outspend the

U.S. in such weaponry. U.S. economic power used in this way broke the deadlock and brought the Soviet leader to agree to mutual nuclear disarmament.

Gorbachev appears to have taken Reagan at his word. Even though it has yet to be perfected, the very concept of Star Wars made the world an infinitely safer place. It was the ultimate bluff, and may still some day become reality.

Likewise, Reagan fought Communism and totalitarianism in the Western Hemisphere wherever he found it. Although there were many reasons for the collapse of Soviet Communism, the policies of the Reagan administration contributed heavily toward it. After his Berlin Wall speech, the people of Eastern Europe began to turn against their Communist puppet overseers. Reagan had scarcely been out of office a year when these countries, one by one, began casting off the yoke of Communism, and became Democratic nations.

Unlike in the past when the Soviets had sent in their army to put down anti-Communist protests, this time it let the countries go, and shortly afterward the Communist Party in Russia itself simply melted away, along with the Union of Soviet Socialist Republics. Remarkably, it was all done peacefully, except in Romania, where the people executed a particularly unpleasant tyrant who had misruled them for years.

In 1989 in East Berlin, joyous citizens rushed through the now-unguarded Brandenburg Gate to reunite with their fellow free Germans. And in what must have been a gratifying moment for Ronald Reagan, they began tearing down the Berlin Wall. Thousands of Germans, men, women, and children, chipped away with hammers, axes, chisels, even pocket knives—any tool available to destroy the hated thing—and all of it was broadcast live on national television, where Reagan could watch.

At last the Cold War was over. The forty-five-year effort to contain Communism had cost America more than 100,000 lives in the Korean and Vietnam Wars and assorted minor conflicts, and an estimated $8 trillion in national treasure. (By way of perspective, $8 trillion is the equivalent of spending $1 billion every single day for the next 8,000 years.) But now the Cold War is history, and Americans can thank Ronald Reagan in large part for that.

★ ★ ★

After Reagan left office, he and Nancy went back to California and their beloved ranch. He was now seventy-eight, and had been the oldest president in U.S. history. It had not been an easy eight years. He had survived an assassin's bullet, battled Congress, and fenced with Soviet leaders. In his final State of the Union speech he said he hoped America was a better place to live in due to his work as president. It was.

He continued to be a popular speaker, until his final public appearance at the funeral of former president Richard Nixon in 1994. Shortly afterward, he was diagnosed with Alzheimer's Disease, an incurable illness that causes the brain cells to die. He was eighty-three years old when he got the news.

His mother had died from the same illness, and after he learned he had it too, Reagan went into his study and hand wrote a letter to the American people:

> I have recently been told that I am one of the millions of Americans who will be afflicted with Alzheimer's Disease.... At the moment I feel just fine. I intend to live the remainder of the years God gives me on this Earth doing the things I've always done.... Unfortunately, as Alzheimer's Disease progresses, the family often bears a heavy burden. I only wish there was some way I could spare Nancy from this painful experience....

> Let me thank you, the American people, for giving me the great honor of allowing me to serve as your president....
>
> I now begin the journey that will lead me to the sunset of my life. I know that for America there will always be a bright dawn ahead.
>
> Thank you, my friends, and may God always bless you.

After that, the Reagans secluded themselves from public life. For a while he was still able to go to the ranch and ride, or take walks, play golf, and go to his office, but as the Alzheimer's progressed it slowly began destroying his memory and his mind. In the last few years, Nancy let very few people see him because, she said, she believed he would have wanted people to remember him as he had been before the disease.

★ ★ ★

Americans are fortunate that they continue to have the same sort of political system devised by the Founding Fathers and adopted by the people in 1787. It is of course, not exactly the same, but rather the same sort. For example, when the Constitution was ratified, women, Native Americans, blacks, and citizens who did not pay property taxes could not vote; U.S. senators were elected by state legislators; and it would have been unthinkable for those aspiring to the presidency to actually conduct national *political campaigns*—let alone ones that cost hundreds of millions of dollars.

The system has adjusted—even strained during the Civil War era—but it has always held. Although George Washington himself warned against them, from the very outset we have had political parties. And since the beginning, the electorate has divided itself mainly between liberals and conservatives—between those who want more government and those who want less. Though their parties have had different names over the years, most American voters today are either Democrats or

Republicans, and every four years since the nation's inception, even in crisis, we have had an orderly transfer of governmental power.

Let's contrast this with, say, Italy, whose government seems to be in constant turmoil. Since the end of World War II in 1945, the United States has had twelve administrations under twelve presidents. In those same sixty-odd years, Italy has had sixty-odd administrations under sixty-odd premiers, expanding and contracting and squabbling constantly.

For over two and a quarter centuries, the system embedded in the Constitution has given America strength and stability that are the envy of the world. Reagan understood this and conducted his presidency accordingly—*for the long run*.

In fact, he knew that the United States was not a "young" nation as people often say—in fact, it is one of the oldest in the world today, from the standpoint of political organization. World War I saw the death of four empires, one of them being replaced by the Communist Empire of Russia, which survived for only seventy years.

Because of the economic turmoil that has recently affected the United States and the rest of the capitalist world, there have been the usual outcries announcing the "death of capitalism." This is nothing new; similar pronouncements were made frequently during the Great Depression. Capitalism is by no means a system without flaws, but it might be useful to describe it, paraphrasing Winston Churchill's famous remark about democracy: "It is the worst form of government—except for all the others that have been tried."

It would be interesting to know what Ronald Reagan would have thought and done in the present economic crisis. It's probably a safe bet that his presence would have had a reassuring effect on the country, much like Franklin Roosevelt had a generation earlier. Reagan was a great believer in capitalism, freedom, and the free market system, and there is no indication he would have considered changing his mind, even in very difficult times. He understood the seas would be stormy at times. After all, he had lived through the Great Depression and World War II.

★ ★ ★

On June 5, 2005, Ronald Reagan passed away at his home in Bel Air, California. He was ninety-three years old.

On June 9, his body was flown to Washington, DC, to lie in state in the Rotunda of the U.S. Capitol, where 104,684 mourners viewed it. On June 11, the funeral service was held at the National Cathedral, attended by many of the world's greatest leaders, including his old opponent, Mikhail Gorbachev.

He was buried in California, at the Ronald W. Reagan Presidential Library & Museum. On his gravestone are inscribed words from a speech he delivered at the dedication of his library:

> I know in my heart that man is good, that what is right will always eventually triumph and there is purpose and worth to each and every life.

During his political career, Reagan was disliked, even reviled, by most of the liberal "intelligentsia" and the media. And today there are still those who belittle his role in Russia's decision to stop pointing their nuclear missiles at the United States, and in the ultimate failure of Soviet Communism.

But there are many others who remember Reagan fondly and gratefully, especially from his record thirty-four network television addresses to the American people. What these Americans recall, no matter their politics—or his—was a man of great bearing, of straight talk, full of good humor and good will. He was a cheerful president, no matter what came his way, though he could at times be angry, as he showed in his speeches about Gorbachev's behavior at the Iceland arms conference, and about the Russian pilot's murder of innocent civilians aboard the South Korean airliner.

Reagan had a clear sense of right and wrong, which infuriated many of the leading academics, intellectuals, and establishment journalists, most of whom still remain convinced that applying such moral convictions to political problems is to be judgmental and simplistic. In contrast, Reagan recognized the deep problems inherent in moral relativism (the mindset that all things are equal and there is no objective right or wrong).

Above all else, Reagan was an American original who had his heartbreaks and his triumphs, and he lived a full, rich, important life and died in his own bed.

He had come a long way, the poor boy from Tampico, Illinois, who never knew he was poor, to noted sportscaster, movie star, president of the Screen Actors Guild, California governor, and president of the United States.

And it was all because he didn't get that job at Montgomery Ward, way back in 1932. At least, that was the way he saw it.

If you ever visit the Reagan Library in Simi Valley, California, you will notice a 9-foot concrete slab monolith near the entrance. On the side that faces West it is painted in colorful graffiti of butterflies and flowers, but its East side remains a drab, stark gray. It is an actual 6,338-pound chunk of the Berlin Wall, sent by the citizens of a grateful Germany who prized it as a symbol of Reagan's "tear down this wall" speech, words that echoed around the earth, a call for freedom for East Germany and the rest of the Communist world.

Of this concrete slab Reagan said, "Let our children and grandchildren come here and see this wall and reflect on what it meant to history. Let them understand that only vigilance and strength will deter tyranny."

And each year they come by the tens of thousands, the school children, and read the words, and look out over the valley where his grave lies close by, just a little to the left and, most fittingly, also facing West.

RONALD REAGAN: OUR 40TH PRESIDENT

READER'S GUIDE

The following questions are designed to enhance your reading experience and to give you an opportunity to talk with other people about *Ronald Reagan: Our 40th President*. Discuss your answers and join the conversation by becoming part of the Regnery Publishing Book Club on Goodreads.com!

QUESTIONS

1. Ronald Reagan grew up poor, and during his life he faced many tough challenges. Yet he didn't let anything stop him from dreaming big and working hard to achieve his goals. What are some challenges you face in working toward your own goals and dreams? How can you work to overcome them?

_____
_____
_____
_____

2. Reagan worked hard in every job he ever had, but he also set aside time to unwind with hobbies he enjoyed—especially horseback riding. What are some ways you "recharge" and have fun, so you have enough energy to work hard to accomplish your goals?

_____
_____
_____
_____
_____

3. Reagan's mother had a powerful influence in shaping his character. How have your parents and mentors taught and inspired you to be the best person you can be?

_____
_____
_____
_____
_____

4. Winston Groom writes that Ronald Reagan gave "everything he had" to his work, because that was his character. What is "character"? Why is strong character important for a good leader?

_____
_____
_____
_____
_____

5. Reagan was known to greet his work and the challenges it presented with cheerfulness and a sense of humor. How do you stay cheerful in your life, even when things aren't going very well? Why are cheerfulness and humor so important in life, especially in a good leader?

_____
_____
_____
_____
_____
_____

6. The media often attacked Reagan. How did he respond? How do you respond when your character is called into question?

_____
_____
_____
_____
_____
_____

Join the conversation online:
Go to Goodreads.com and search for
Regnery Publishing Book Club

BIBLIOGRAPHY

Adler, Bill, ed. *The Uncommon Wisdom of Ronald Reagan: A Portrait in His Own Words.* Boston: Little, Brown & Company, 1996.

Billingsley, Kenneth Lloyd. *Hollywood Party: How Communism Seduced the American Film Industry in the 1930s and 1940s.* Rocklin, CA: Forum, 1998.

Brinkley, Douglas, ed. *The Reagan Diaries.* New York: Harper Collins, 2007.

D'Souza, Dinesh. *Ronald Reagan. How an Ordinary Man Became an Extraordinary leader.* New York: Simon & Schuster, 1997.

Eubanks, Steve. *Quotable Reagan: Words of Wit, Wisdom, & Statesmanship By and About Ronald Reagan, America's Great Communicator.* Nashville: TowleHouse Publishing, 2001.

The Greatest Speeches of Ronald Reagan. A NewsMax.com Book. West Palm Beach, FL, 2001.

Greider, William. "The Education of David Stockman." *The Atlantic Monthly*, December 1981.

Humes, James C. *The Wit & Wisdom of Ronald Reagan.* Washington, DC: Regnery Publishing, Inc., 2007.

Morris, Edmund. *Dutch: A Memoir of Ronald Reagan.* New York: Random House, 1999.

Noonan, Peggy. *When Character Was King: A Story of Ronald Reagan.* New York: Penguin Books, 2001.

Radosh, Ronald, and Allis Radosh. *Red Star Over Hollywood: The Film Colony's Long Romance with the Left.* New York: Encounter Books, 2006.

Reagan, Maureen. *First Father, First Daughter: A Memoir.* Boston: Little Brown & Co., 1989.

Reagan, Michael with Joe Hyams. *On the Outside Looking In.* New York: Zebra Books, 1998.

Reagan, Ronald. *An American Life.* New York: Pocket Books, 1990.

——— with Richard G. Hubler. *Ronald Reagan's Own Story: Where's the Rest of Me?* New York: Karz-Segil, 1981.

Skinner, Kiron K., Annelise Anderson, and Martin Anderson, eds. *Reagan: A Life in Letters.* New York: Free Press, 2003.

———, eds. *Stories in His Own Hand: The Everyday Wisdom of Ronald Reagan.* New York: Free Press, 2001.

Wirthlin, Dick with Wynton C. Hall. *The Greatest Communicator: What Ronald Reagan Taught Me About Politics, Leadership and Life.* Hoboken, NJ: John Wiley & Sons, 2004.

INDEX

1972 Olympic Games in Munich, 133

A

ABC News, 94
Afghanistan, 111
Air America, 117
air traffic controllers' strike, 100–1
Al Jazeera, 133
Allies, the, 53
Alzheimer's Disease, 44, 144
American Federation of Labor (AFL), 52
Angola, 111
Arnow, Max, 38
atomic weapons (*see also*: nuclear missiles), 2, 91, 122, 142
Austria, 53

Axis Powers, 34

B

B-1 bomber, 112
Bad Man, The, 42
Baltic States, 53
Barry, Philip, 38
Barrymore, Lionel, 42
Bedtime for Bonzo, 74
Beery, Wallace, 42–43
Beirut, 104–5
Bellamann, Henry, 44
Bergman, Ingrid, 73
Berlin, 125–27, 133
    East Berlin, 143
Berlin Wall, 125, 143, 148
big government, 31, 79–80, 137, 142

blacklist, 51, 64–65, 75
Bogart, Humphrey, 40, 51, 65
Boland Amendment, 131
Boll Weevil Democrats, 93
Brady, James, 98
Brandenburg Gate, 125–26, 143
Breslin, Jimmy, 94
Bridges, Harry, 55
Broadway, 19, 71, 76
Broderick, Helen, 51
Brother Rat, 40
Brown, Pat, 81
Buchanan, James, 1
Burbank, 39, 71
bureaucracy, 31–32, 49, 83, 88
Bush, George H. W., 132, 138

C

Cagney, James, 39–40, 45, 51, 65
Caldicott, Dr. Helen, 116–17
California, 37, 39, 63, 81–85, 90, 99, 102, 113, 144, 147–48
California National Guard, 84
Cambodia, 111
Camp David, 101–2
capitalism (*see also*: free market), 58, 136–37, 146
Carter, Jimmy, 7–8, 89–90, 93, 111, 130
Castro, Fidel, 107–9
CBS, 28, 103

Chicago, 9, 12, 27–29, 32–33, 37–38
China, 5, 79, 110
Christ Church, 20
Churchill, Winston, 53, 146
City of Hope Hospital, 73
Civil Service, 49
Civil War, 42, 57, 145
Cleaver, Margaret, 20–21, 25, 29, 33, 68
Clifford, Clark, 94
Coburn, Charles, 44
Cohn, Harry, 122
Cold War, 6, 53–54, 110, 143–44
   Containment policy and, 110
   détente policy and, 111
   Peaceful Coexistence policy and, 110
Comintern (*see also*: Communist *Internationale*), 54
Communism, 5, 53–54, 59, 61–62, 65, 67, 78–80, 110–12, 130, 135–36, 142–43
   attempted infiltration of U.S. and, 60
   expansionism of, 65, 121
   HICCASP and, 63, 67
   Karl Marx and, 58, 78–79
   labor unions and, 54, 60
   in motion picture industry, 53, 65

Index

Soviet Communism, 4, 7, 59, 111, 143, 147
Communist *Internationale* (*see also*: Comintern), 54
Communist Party, 60–61, 65, 80, 135, 143
Congress, 31, 73, 88, 92, 94, 108, 111, 119, 123, 130–32, 138, 142, 144
Constitution, U.S., 64, 79, 145–46
Contras, 130–32
Cooper, Gary, 129
Cuba, 5, 79, 107–9, 130
Cuban Missile Crisis, 108, 130
Cubs, 32–33, 37–38
Culver City, 48
Cummings, Robert, 44
Czechoslovakia, 53, 135

D

Da Silva, Howard, 60
Davenport, 29, 32
Davis, Nancy. *See*: Reagan, Nancy
De Cordova, Fred, 74
de Havilland, Olivia, 40, 61, 63, 65, 70
Dean, Dizzy, 33
Dell computers, 137
Dell, Michael, 110
DeMille, Cecil B., 70
democracy, 62, 65, 130, 132, 146

Democratic Party, 30, 81
Des Moines, 32, 34, 38
Detroit, 23
Disciples of Christ, 22
Dixon, 13–14, 17, 21, 23–24, 27–28, 30, 34, 49
Dixon High School, 19, 29, 42, 50
Donaldson, Sam, 94

E

East Germany, 127, 148
economy
  Communism and, 78
  of Soviet Union, 135
  of United States, 5, 89–91, 141
Engels, Friedrich, 58
Ethiopia, 111
Eureka College, 21–24, 27, 30, 41–42, 50, 91

F

Federal Bureau of Investigation (FBI), 60, 66
fellow travelers, 60, 63
Fifth Amendment, 64
Flynn, Errol, 40, 42, 72
Ford, Gerald, 6–7, 89
Ford Motor Company, 23
Fort Mason, 47
Fort Roach, 48–49
Foster, Jodie, 100

Founding Fathers, 89, 145
Frazer, B. J., 19
free market (*see also*: capitalism), 146

G

Gable, Clark, 73, 129
Gaddafi, Muammar, 133–34
Garfield, John, 60
gasoline, 5
Gates, Bill, 110
General Electric Company 77–78, 80, 83
General Electric Theater, 77–78
Geneva Conference, 122
George Washington University Hospital, 97
Germany, 53, 78, 125, 127, 148
Gettysburg Address, 125
Ghost Mountain, 72
Gipp, George ("the Gipper"), 41–42
glasnost, 135
Gone with the Wind, 61, 70
Gorbachev, Mikhail, 121–24, 127, 134–38, 142–43, 147
    Soviet economy and, 135
    Strategic Defense Initiative (SDI) and, 124
Grant, Cary, 40, 51–52
Great Britain, 6, 53, 134
Great Depression, the, 1, 24, 27, 49, 58, 67, 146
Grenada, 107–9, 111, 130

Group Theater, 54

H

Harvard University, 17–18, 81
Hasty Heart, The, 68
Hayden, Sterling, 60
Hayes, Rutherford B., 3
Hayworth, Rita, 68
Hezbollah, 105
Hinckley, John, 99
Hitler, Adolf, 34, 53
Holden, William, 76, 129
Holiday, 38
Hollywood, 3, 23, 29, 37, 39, 41–42, 48–55, 59–61, 63–65, 67, 69, 72–73, 76–78, 94, 99
    blacklisting and, 51, 64–65, 75
    Communism and, 54–55, 59–61, 64, 78
    Studio System and, 40, 69, 77
    unions and, 50–53, 61, 63, 65
Hollywood Independent Citizens Committee of the Arts, Sciences, and Professions (HICCASP), 61–63
Hope, Bob, 44
"The House of the Future," 77
House of Representatives, 92–93, 123
House Un-American Activities Committee (HUAC), 63–66, 67
Hungary, 53, 135

Index

I
Iceland, 123–24
Iceland arms conference, 147
inflation, 4–5, 89, 141
intercontinental ballistic missiles (ICBMs), 119
interest rates, 5, 89, 141
Iran, 8, 89, 105, 131–33
    U.S. embassy hostage situation and, 8, 89
Iran-Contra Affair, 132–33
Irish Potato Famine, 10
Iron Curtain, 4, 53
Islam, 5, 8, 89, 131, 133
Israel, 103–4, 131, 133
    Palestinian exiles and, 104
    Palestinian prisoners of, 131
Ivy League, 18

J
Japan, 34, 45, 48–49, 102, 120
Jobs, Steve, 110
Joint Chiefs of Staff, 114, 134
Jurges, Billy, 33

K
Kennedy, John F., 92, 108, 125
Khomeini, Ayatollah, 8
Khrushchev, Nikita, 126
Kings Row, 44–45
Knute Rockne, All American, 42–43
Korea, 6, 110
Korean War, 100
Kremlin, the, 121

L
Lake Geneva, 122
Laos, 111
Las Vegas, 77
Last Outpost, The, 74
Lawrence Livermore National Laboratory, 113
Lawson, Howard W., 62–63
League of Nations, 34
Lebanon, 104–5, 107, 132
Lenin, Vladimir, 59, 121
LeRoy, Mervyn, 75
Libya, 133–34
Lincoln, Abraham, 1, 57, 125
Little Brown Church, 76
Lockerbie bombing, 134
Los Angeles, 37, 40, 82, 87
Louisa, 74
Love Is on the Air, 40
Lowell wildlife sanctuary, 17
Lupino, Ida, 73–74

M
MacArthur, Peter ("Pete"), 29, 32
Marine One, 101
Marx Brothers, 51
Marx, Karl, 58, 78–79
Mayer, Louis B., 122
Meet the Press, 82

Meiklejohn, Bill, 38
Metro-Goldwyn Mayer (MGM), 61, 75–76
MiG fighters, 133
military, Cuban, 107, 109
military, Soviet, 7, 90–91, 110, 135
military, U.S., 5, 7–8, 40, 49, 90–91, 111–14, 120, 131, 142
Monte Carlo, 68
Montgomery, Robert, 129
Montgomery Ward, 28, 51, 72, 148
Mozambique, 111
Mrs. Miniver, 45
Mussolini, Benito, 34
Mutually Assured Destruction (MAD), 6–7, 91
MX "Peacekeeper," 112, 120, 142

N

National Security Council, 132
Native Americans, 145
NBC, 28–29, 32, 82
New Deal, 50
New York Times, 112
Nicaragua, 108, 111, 130–32
Nixon, Richard, 81, 110–11, 131, 144
Noonan, Peggy, 99, 103
North American Aerospace Defense Command (NORAD), 113
North Korea, 79
North, Oliver, 131
Notre Dame University, 112

nuclear freeze, 115–16
nuclear missiles (*see also*: atomic weapons), 121, 134, 147
 in Cuba, 107
 defense against, 124
 negotiations surrounding, 121–25, 134–36
 nuclear freeze movement, 116
 reduction of, 119, 122–24, 136
 Soviet development of, 6, 91, 114, 134
 Soviet superiority in, 115
 U.S. development of, 91, 112–13, 142
nuclear war, 6, 111, 114, 120, 130

O

O'Brien, Pat, 41
O'Neill, Tip, 92–93, 112, 119, 137
Organization of Eastern Caribbean States, 107–8
Oval Office, 1, 116, 139

P

Pacific Palisades, 76–77
Parsons, Louella, 41
Pearl Harbor, 45, 125
perestroika, 135–36
Pershing missiles, 115, 122
Phoenix, 76
Pidgeon, Walter, 129
Pinkos, 60

Poland, 53, 135
political classes, 135
Powell, Dick, 51, 129

R

Rains, Claude, 44
Reagan, Jack, 10–13, 17, 20–21, 24, 30–31, 40–41
Reagan, Maureen, 41, 68, 99, 115–17
Reagan, Michael, 41, 68, 99, 115–17
Reagan, Nancy, 75–76, 87, 99, 101–3, 116–17, 121, 129, 136, 144–45
Reagan, Neil ("Moon"), 9–13, 21, 24, 39
Reagan, Nelle, 11–12, 20, 24, 43–44, 72, 144
Reagan, Patti, 76, 115–17
Reagan, Ron, Jr., 76, 115–17
Reagan, Ronald W.
  assassination attempt on, 101, 133
  Berlin Wall speech of, 125–27, 143, 148
  big government and, 31, 79–80, 137, 142, 148
  Communism and, 4, 62, 65, 67, 78–80, 110–12, 136, 142–43, 147
  death of, 117, 147
  as "Dutch," 9–15, 19, 23–24, 43, 72
  early life of, 9–25
  education of, 16–25
  "Evil Empire" and, 107–18, 127
  family life of, 40–41, 68, 76, 116–18
  foreign policy of, 142
  as governor of California, 29, 81, 83–85, 87, 90, 113, 116, 148
  as "the Great Communicator," 3
  in Hollywood, 3, 23, 29, 38–45, 67, 69, 72–74, 95, 99
  involvement with SAG, 51–52, 65, 73, 75–76
  marriages of, 41, 68, 76, 99, 115
  media and, 4, 92, 94, 108–9, 112, 115, 124, 127, 129, 132, 147
  Mikhail Gorbachev and, 122–24, 127, 134–38, 142–43, 147
  military rebuilding of, 90–91, 111–12
  military service of, 34, 40, 45, 47–55, 59
  political conversion of, 57–66
  as radio announcer, 27–35, 40
  taxes and, 70, 91, 101, 141
Reaganomics, 92
Reds, 60
Republican National Committee, 117
Republican party, 57–58, 81, 89, 98, 117
Roach, Hal, 48
Robinson, Edward G., 65

Rock River, 17, 23, 27
Rockne, Knute, 41–42
Ronald Reagan Presidential Library, 19, 147–48
Roosevelt, Franklin D., 1, 30–32, 50, 57, 125, 146
Roosevelt, James ("Jimmy"), 61–62
Roosevelt, Theodore, 142
Russia, 5, 6, 53, 58–59, 61–62, 64, 91, 103, 108–9, 112–13, 115, 119–22, 124, 127, 134–36, 138, 142–43, 146–48

S

San Fernando Valley, 76
San Francisco, 47, 55
Sandinistas, 130
Santa Barbara, 87
Santa Fe Trail, 42, 72
Santa Monica Mountains, 76
Santa Ynez Mountains, 87
Schary, Dore, 61
Screen Actors Guild (SAG), 51–52, 65, 73, 75–76
Secret Service, 97–99, 103, 138
Senate, 93–94, 117
She's Working Her Way Through College, 74
Sheridan, Ann, 44
Shultz, George, 124
Simi Valley, 148
socialism, 58, 78, 80

South Bend, 44
South Korean jetliner incident, 120, 148
South Vietnam, 6, 111
Soviet Union
  Cold War and, 53, 110
  collapse of, 142–43
  Communism and, 79, 130
  Cuba and, 107–8
  détente and, 111
  economy of, 109, 135
  espionage and, 60, 64
  as Evil Empire, 112
  expansion of, 54, 64, 90
  Hollywood and, 53, 59
  MAD doctrine and, 114
  military buildup of, 142
  Muslims and, 104
  nuclear arms negotiations and, 121–25, 134–37
  nuclear arsenal of, 91
  Star Wars and, 120, 123
  world domination and, 5
SS-20 missiles, 114
St. George's University School of Medicine, 108
St. Louis Cardinals, 33
Stalin, Joseph, 59
"Star Wars." *See:* Strategic Defense Initiative (SDI)
Stewart, Jimmy, 73
stock market crash of 1929, 24, 58

Storm Warning, 74
Strategic Defense Initiative (SDI), 107–18, 120, 120–25, 136, 142–43
strikes
    of air traffic controllers, 100
    at California colleges, 84
    at Eureka College, 22–23, 50
    in Hollywood, 51–53, 54
Studio System, 40, 69, 77
supply-side economics, 92

T

Tampico, 9, 12, 14, 148
Tau Kappa Alpha (TKE), 22
taxes, 70, 80, 84, 88, 91, 101, 141, 145
Taylor, Robert, 38, 129
Teller, Edward, 113
Temple, Shirley, 71
Tennessee Valley Authority (TVA), 80
terrorism, 8, 134
That Hagen Girl, 71–73
Time, 133
Tip Top ranch, 88
Tokyo, 48–49
Tornado, 9
totalitarianism, 143
Tracy, Spencer, 129
trickle-down economics, 92
Truman, Harry S., 1, 100, 110

Trumbo, Dalton, 61–62
Tucker, Sophie, 76
Turner, Lana, 68

U

U.S. Army 14th Cavalry Regiment, 34
U.S. Communist Party, 80
U.S. Department of Education, 88
U.S. Department of Justice, 69
U.S. Marines, 105, 107, 109
U.S. national debt, 138
U.S. Treasury, 92
Union of Soviet Socialist Republics. *See:* Soviet Union
unions, 50–55, 60, 63, 65, 78, 80
United Nations, 103
Universal Pictures, 73
University of California, 82, 84–85, 113
University of Michigan, 89
USA Today, 94
USS *New Jersey*, 105

V

Variety, 41, 72
veto power, 94, 138
Vietnam, 6, 82, 84, 110–11, 144
Vietnam War, 82, 84, 144
Virginia Military Institute (VMI), 40

W

Waldorf Statement, 64
War Department, 45
Warner Brothers, 38–41, 43, 45, 51, 69, 71–73, 82
Warner, Jack, 71, 122
Washington, George, 2, 4, 97, 99, 101, 145
Washington Post, 132
Watergate scandal, 132
Weinberger, Caspar, 83
welfare, 30–31, 49, 81
WGN, 28
Where's the Rest of Me?, 48
White House, 1, 4, 72, 92, 97, 99–101, 103, 115, 117, 129–30, 137–38, 141
White House Rose Garden, 100
White Sox, 32
WHO, 32, 37, 39
Wood, Sam, 45
Works Progress Administration, 30
World of Chiropractic (WOC), 29–30, 32
World War I, 13, 146
World War II, 1, 5–6, 31, 45, 64, 103–4, 110, 120, 146–47
Wrigley Field, 33, 37
Wyman, Jane, 40, 67, 76, 99, 115

Y

Yale University, 17–18, 117
Yankee Doodle Dandy, 45
Yemen, 111
YMCA, 11, 18

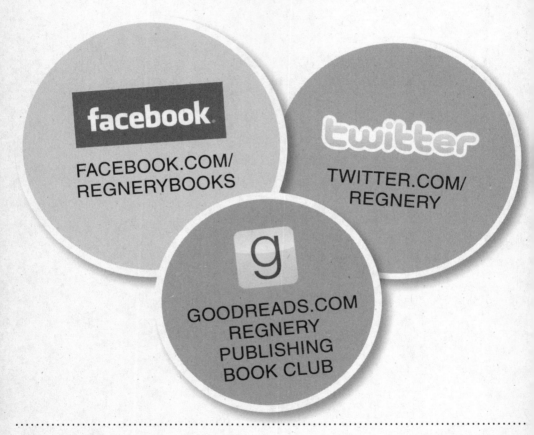